Studies
Writing & Rhetoric

IN 1980, THE CONFERENCE ON COLLEGE COMPOSITION AND COM-
MUNICATION perceived a need for publishing opportunities for
monographs that were too lengthy for publication in its journal and
too short for the typical publication of scholarly books by The National Council of Teachers of English. A series called Studies in
Writing and Rhetoric was conceived, and a Publication Committee
established.

Monographs to be considered for publication may be speculative,
theoretical, historical, or analytical studies; research reports; or
other works contributing to a better understanding of writing, including interdisciplinary studies or studies in disciplines related to
composing. The SWR series will exclude textbooks, unrevised dis-
sertations, book-length manuscripts, course syllabi, lesson plans,
and collections of previously published material.

Any teacher-writer interested in submitting a work for publication in this series should send either a prospectus and sample manuscript or a full manuscript to the NCTE Coordinator of Professional
Publications, 1111 Kenyon Road, Urbana, IL 61801. Accompanied
by sample manuscript, a prospectus should contain a rationale, a
definition of readership within the CCCC constituency, comparison
with related publications, an annotated table of contents, an esti-
mate of length in double-spaced 8½ x 11 sheets, and the date by
which full manuscript can be expected. Manuscripts should be in
the range of 100 to 170 typed manuscript pages.

The works that have been published in this series serve as models
for future SWR monographs.

Paul O'Dea
NCTE Coordinator of Professional Publications

Invention as
a Social Act

Karen Burke LeFevre

With a foreword by FRANK J. D'ANGELO

Published for the Conference on College
Composition and Communication

SOUTHERN ILLINOIS UNIVERSITY PRESS
Carbondale and Edwardsville

Production of works in this series has been partly funded by the Conference on College Composition and Communication of the National Council of Teachers of English.

Printed in the United States of America
Edited by Margaret E. Sattler
Designed by Design for Publishing, Inc., Bob Nance
production supervised by Natalia Nadraga

92   91   4   3

Library of Congress Cataloging-in-Publication Data

LeFevre, Karen Burke.
   Invention as a social act.

   (Studies in writing & rhetoric)
   "Published for the Conference on College
Composition and Communication."
   Bibliography: p.
   1. Invention (Rhetoric)—Social aspects.
I. Conference on College Composition and Communication
(U.S.)   II. Title.   III. Series.
PN221.L44   1987   808   86-15437
ISBN 0-8093-1328-6

To Anne Burke and to the memory of Paul L. Burke

Contents

Foreword

Frank J. D'Angelo

INVENTION AS A SOCIAL ACT IS AN IMPORTANT AND TIMELY STUDY.
It connects, on the one hand, to current work in literary theory and,
on the other, to work in composition theory. Traditional literary theory assumes a solitary, autonomous author who is solely responsible
for the mode of existence of a literary work. But in his essay "What
Is an Author?" (*Partisan Review*, 42 [1975]), Michel Foucault argues
that the concept of the author as one who authorizes, authenticates,
originates, brings into being, creates, or invents a text is of relatively recent origin. There was a time, Foucault writes, when literary narratives, poems, and plays were composed and circulated
without the question of authorship ever being raised. In fact, the
concept of the author may be nothing more than a convenient fiction. "One comes to the conclusion that the author's name does not
refer to a real person but that it exceeds the limits of the texts, that
it organizes them, that it reveals their mode of being, or at least
characterizes them. Though it clearly points to the existence of certain texts, it also refers to their status within a society and within a
culture. . . . The function of an author is thus characteristic of the
mode of existence, circulation, and operation of certain discourses
within society."

Like traditional literary theory, traditional composition theory
depicts an ideal writer, isolated from the social world, who works
alone, using various kinds of compositional strategies to plan,
organize, and produce a text. But in a recent *College English* article, "The Ecology of Writing" (April 1986), Marilyn Cooper argues
that this image of the solitary composer is a myth. "Language and

texts," she asserts, "are not simply the means by which individuals discover and communicate information, but are essentially social activities, dependent on social structures and processes not only in their interpretive but also in their constructive phases." It is in the context of this kind of criticism of the concept of the author that Karen LeFevre's study might more fruitfully be understood.

In *Invention as a Social Act*, Karen LeFevre contends that American composition theory and pedagogy of the nineteenth and twentieth centuries is founded on the "Platonic" view that invention is a solitary act in which the individual, drawing upon innate knowledge and mental structures, searches for the truth, using introspective self-examination and heuristic methods of various kinds. Composition favors this view of composing, states LeFevre, because of the influence of traditional literary studies on the teaching of composition, the persistence of the romantic myth of the inspired writer, and the effects of capitalism and individualism on the concept of invention. Although this view is valuable in emphasizing internal resources and in showing how invention relates to the composing process, it depicts invention as a closed, one-way system; assumes and promotes the concept of the atomic self as inventor; abstracts the writer from society; neglects studies of writers in social contexts; and fails to acknowledge that invention is collaborative.

Invention is best understood as a social act, LeFevre reasons, even when the agent is an individual. However, more often than we realize, agency may more appropriately be attributed to two or more people who collaborate to create something new. As a social act, invention has four aspects. First, invention is social even when the agent is a single individual because the inventing "self" is socially influenced. Second, human agents always act dialectically—in the context of their interconnections with others and the socioculture. Third, although invention is initiated by an agent, the inventor always requires the presence of an "other"—either the rhetor himself or herself as *internalized other* or a perceived audience of *actual others*. Finally, invention as a social act has classical precedents. These include Socratic dialogue, the rhetorical enthymeme for which the audience must supply the premises, the three kinds of Aristotelian proof which presuppose an audience that may not accept them, and the concept of ethos which arises from the relationship between the individual and the community.

After discussing how invention can be perceived as a social act,

LeFevre presents the reader with four perspectives on invention. (1) The *Platonic perspective*, based on Plato's myth of the soul, considers invention a private activity by an individual who possesses innate knowledge to be recollected and expressed or innate cognitive structures to be projected onto the world. (2) The *internal dialogic perspective*, based on Freud's model of the psyche, maintains that invention involves an internal dialogue or dialectic with an inner "self" which, like Freud's superego, serves as a monitor and a bridge to the rest of the social world. (3) The *collaborative perspective* is based on George Herbert Mead's contention that meaning is not privately constructed in an individual's consciousness, but is generated by symbolic gestures that call for a response in others. (4) Finally, the *social collective perspective* is based on Emile Durkheim's theory that a collective force or "mind" permeates a society and acts, often through established institutions and conventions, to influence the attitudes, behaviors, and inventions of members of social groups.

In a view of invention as a social act, language provides an important foundation. Is it appropriate to regard language as an active force in thinking and inventing, LeFevre asks? To what extent is the use of language in invention a social act relying on a shared system of symbols developed and used by a language community? Language is not just the passive copying of an extralinguistic reality, LeFevre answers, but an active force in constituting reality. Humans do not confront reality directly, but through language and other symbol systems. But people do not invent the language they use; they absorb it from others in a culture. Language is thus a dialectic between the individual and the social realms.

LeFevre concludes her study with some important directions for writers, researchers, scholars, and teachers. These include studying writing in social contexts, taking note of various kinds of people who affect invention (editors, colleagues, spouses, collaborators), encouraging group authorship and other collaborative activities, increasing flexible work space for group activities, and integrating writing with learning across the curriculum. LeFevre's analysis of traditional approaches to rhetorical invention, her proposed model of invention as a social act, and her discussion of the implications of this model for the teaching of writing constitute a significant contribution to our understanding of the process of writing and open up new research possibilities for teachers and scholars.

ACKNOWLEDGMENTS

MY PERSONAL EXPERIENCE IN CARRYING OUT THIS STUDY HAS strengthened my theoretical conviction that invention is best understood as a social act. In *The Philosophy of Literary Form*, Kenneth Burke describes an "'unending conversation' that is going on at the point in history when we are born." This conversation, which gives rise to materials for the dramatic process of history, precedes us and continues after we depart: "You listen for a while," Burke says, "until you decide that you have caught the tenor of the argument; then you put in your oar." Broadly applied, Burke's metaphor alludes to birth and death, but it aptly describes as well one's part in a community of discourse or in a particular debate within that community. In the chapters on invention that follow, as I "put in my oar," I attempt to identify those points at which the voices of others—those necessary others whose words I have read, and those with whom I have spoken and thought and worked—are particularly evident. In addition, general acknowledgments are in order here.

Above all I wish to acknowledge gratefully the significant contributions of S. Michael Halloran, whose influence is present in and beyond these pages, as a friend, a critic of visions and revisions, a source of ideas, and a partner in fruitful and continuing conversations. By being available to respond to and amplify ideas in their early stages, he invited invention.

Others have been very helpful at various stages as this work progressed. Lee Odell provided careful readings of two previous drafts of the manuscript, and in doing so, raised many thought-provoking questions. Richard K. Worthington made valuable comments from a political scientist's perspective, and I have particularly appreciated his optimism as this study evolved. Merrill Whitburn gave constant encouragement and helped me find ways to make time to complete the necessary revisions. Douglas Washburn provided a close reading of sections of the manuscript, and T. J. Larkin devoted many hours to discussions about language, philosophy, and social theory. Members of the Publications Committee for the Studies in Writing and Rhetoric Series provided useful suggestions for revision. In his role as NCTE director of publications, Paul O'Dea was helpful and gracious, putting into practice a statement he once made in a letter extending a deadline: "Professional acts should be social acts as well."

Others have played less direct but nonetheless important parts in making my work possible. Philip Booth and Ralph Ciancio, both former teachers of mine and continuing friends, have had little to do with what is said in these pages but a good deal to do with their being written at all, by virtue of their advice and faith over many years. Richard E. Young's exemplary work first drew me to the topic of rhetorical invention, and I feel fortunate to have had the benefit of the "problem-finding" he has accomplished for contemporary rhetoricians interested in invention. Whenever you write a book, Gertrude Stein has said, you need to have "someone say yes to it." I have been fortunate in having generous colleagues from Canada to "say yes" to what I was attempting: Anthony Paré, Richard M. Coe, and James A. Reither. By debating points, suggesting readings, and directing me to other people with like interests, each has helped me test ideas and bring this work to completion.

I am grateful as well to the friends and relatives who have helped my family and me in various ways, providing dinners and child care, pleasure and understanding. In particular I thank the late Paul L. Burke, Anne Burke, Russell LeFevre, Allie Stickney, David Wagner, Lynn Stillman, Jim Stillman, Barbara Murphy, and Roman Kokodyniak. Most of all, I owe a great debt to Jim and Colby LeFevre, who probably do *not* think that invention is a social act, since the process of invention meant that I spent many hours and days away from them over the past three years. Jim willingly spent a year commuting and devoted much time beyond that to chores and child care so that I could take time to complete this work. Somehow he has managed to remain sympathetic and good-humored throughout. I am very much aware of his presence between all these lines, and I thank him for the extraordinary things he has done.

Invention as a Social Act

1

Introduction

IN CONTEMPORARY COMPOSITION THEORY, RHETORICAL INVEN-
tion is commonly viewed as the private act of an individual writer
for the particular event of producing a text, typically a theme or an
essay. Models of prewriting and invention cited in composition textbooks and articles are frequently based on what I will refer to as a
Platonic view of rhetorical invention. They conceive of invention as
individual introspection: ideas are created in the mind of an atomistic individual and then expressed to the rest of the world. Invention is regarded as an unfolding, a manifestation of an individual's ideas, feelings, voice, personality, and patterns of thought. Like
Plato's metaphor of the soul whose wings unfold when it is reminded
of the ideal forms it once beheld, this view of invention stresses the
recovery and expression of an individual's inner (and perhaps latent)
voice or innate cognitive structures. Truth is sought through purely
individual efforts.

While a Platonic view of invention encourages self-expression and
reassures writers of their inner resources, it sketches an incomplete
picture of what happens when writers invent, and it may unduly
constrain the development of processes of invention. This study argues that rhetorical invention is better understood as a social act, in
which an individual who is at the same time a social being interacts
in a distinctive way with society and culture to create something.
Viewed in this way, rhetorical invention becomes an act that may
involve speaking and writing, and that at times involves more than
one person; it is furthermore an act initiated by writers and completed by readers, extending over time through a series of transactions and texts. While others are thus implicated in invention, say-

ing that invention is best understood as a social act neither denies an individual the possibility of creating something original nor frees her from personal responsibility for what she invents.

The social aspects of rhetorical invention are significant, constituting much more than a mere setting or environment within which the creative acts of individuals occur. Invention may first of all be seen as social in that the self that invents is, according to many modern theorists, not merely socially influenced but even socially constituted. Furthermore, one invents largely by means of language and other symbol systems, which are socially created and shared. Invention often occurs through the socially learned process of an internal dialogue with an imagined other, and the invention process is enabled by an internal social construct of audience, which supplies premises and structures of beliefs that guide the writer. Invention becomes explicitly social when writers involve other people as collaborators, or as reviewers whose comments aid invention, or as "resonators" who nourish the development of ideas. To create discourses such as contracts, treaties, and business proposals, two or more writers *must* invent together. Finally, invention is powerfully influenced by social collectives, such as institutions, bureaucracies, and governments, which transmit expectations and prohibitions, encouraging certain ideas and discouraging others.

Before exploring what it means to adopt a social perspective, I must describe the view of the function and scope of rhetorical invention that forms the basis for this study. In contrast to what E. W. Harrington has called a "narrow" view regarding invention as a scheme for remembering or locating topics to apply to an immediate argument, I emphasize what Harrington calls a "broad" view of invention: "the problem of finding [or making, I would add] sound subject matter, of seeking to find all relationships that might exist between what could be known about the situation and the immediate problem to be discussed, in short, the attempt to be wise as well as eloquent."[1] Conceiving of rhetorical invention as a search for wisdom—a search that involves analyzing subjects, audiences, and problems as well as generating and judging ideas, information, propositions, and lines of reasoning—aligns rhetorical invention closely with inquiry or with "invention" in the generic sense: the creation of what is new in any discipline or endeavor. Rhetorical invention becomes a species of invention in general.

While my primary aim is to gain a more comprehensive understanding of what we have come to think of as rhetorical invention, I have found that it is not easy and not always desirable to separate rhetorical invention from the other species of invention. The act of inventing—which may involve remembering or finding or actively creating something—relates to the process of inquiry, to creativity, to poetic and aesthetic invention. While these terms are not synonymous, neither are they totally distinct. Like the historian or the scientist, the poet or fiction writer presumably seeks truth and hopes to be believed. In poetic as well as rhetorical invention (or, if you prefer, in a rhetorical view of poetic invention), the writer wishes to be wise as well as eloquent. If we try to draw sharp boundaries here, we are faced with difficult questions: Does rhetorical invention apply to nonfiction and not to fiction or poetry? Is it used exclusively for instrumental rather than expressive ends? Does it involve "ordinary" rather than "literary" language? To answer such questions, we are apt to formulate tenuous distinctions that become useless as quickly as they are made.

In fact, the contemporary trend has been to broaden rather than restrict the territory to which the term "rhetorical invention" might apply. The 1971 Report of the Speech Communication Association's Committee on the Nature of Rhetorical Invention recognizes and supports this trend. The report proposes as valuable areas for inquiry, for instance, the "relationships between rhetorical and aesthetic invention" and "the modes of discovery in all areas"; it advocates research to develop "a theory of the structures of inquiry, deciding, and choosing" and research "to examine the relationship between 'rhetorical invention' and 'creativity.'"[2] This expanded treatment of rhetorical invention moves it away from its traditionally close association with persuasive discourse dealing with probable matters in a given situation, guiding it toward a more general view. "It is important," the report concludes, "in an age in which fixed forms—whether in metaphysics, art, poetics, cultural patterns, and so forth—are under attack, to look at the world from the perspective of invention, taken as the generation of something new. . . . Invention (used now as the generic term) becomes in this context a productive human thrust into the unknown."[3]

To study the relationship of rhetorical invention to invention in its generic sense, two general approaches may be taken, either of which may be instructive depending on the circumstances and objectives. First, we could look through the lens of rhetorical invention—considered, for the moment, as the discovery of what there is to be known and said, for the traditionally rhetorical purpose of persuasion in a given situation—to see how this perspective helps us to understand invention when it occurs in any discipline or endeavor. Taking this approach, for example, we might analyze the rhetorical situation of Watson and Crick's announcement of the discovery of the structure of DNA, attending to the interrelationships of inventor, reader, and text, as well as to the nature of the arguments invented to persuade the scientific community of the accuracy of this new explanation.[4]

A second approach investigating the interrelationships of rhetorical invention and invention as a generic activity would instead focus on invention as it occurs in and across various fields such as physics or electrical engineering or art to see what the modes of inventing characteristic to those fields may show us that would benefit the study and teaching of rhetorical invention. Using this approach, we might investigate the process of inquiry that Watson and Crick employed to discover the double helical structure of DNA. Our aim in this instance would be to see if understanding the invention process in science better enables us to grasp what happens when writers and speakers invent in situations that are conventionally regarded as more paradigmatically rhetorical.

The first approach, then, emphasizes how rhetorical invention informs our understanding of invention in general; the second, how the study of invention in general informs our understanding of rhetorical invention. In this study I will emphasize the second approach, drawing on theories and examples of processes of invention in a variety of fields to glean from them whatever helps us to understand the social elements that are central to the generation of what is new. I have chosen this approach in part because I think that composition studies too often tend to treat rhetorical invention as an isolated phenomenon occurring in the composition class, while overlooking the import of "invention" in its broader sense. While the first approach outlined here is being used to good effect to bring rhetorical criticism to arenas from which it was previously excluded (such as science and technology), the second approach has not yet been sufficiently tried and tested. If rhetoric is truly to be regarded as an interdisciplinary, epistemic enterprise—as the creation and communication of knowledge through symbolic activity—then we must not only bring rhetoric to bear on other fields, but we must also bring those fields to bear on our understanding of rhetoric.

Having noted the contrast between invention in its generic and rhetorical senses, I will not continue to maintain the separation of these terms each time I refer to the process of generating what one comes to know and what constitutes the substance of discourse. Since part of my aim is to suggest that invention processes are not always as different as they are sometimes made to seem, it would be counterproductive to use terminology that calls attention to their differences. In general, then, I will simply use the term "invention," except when a qualification or elaboration seems necessary for the sake of emphasis or clarity. It is true, however, that in light of the expanding scope that is being allotted (here and elsewhere) to rhetorical invention, one task of future scholars will be to develop new classifications and definitions that do enable us to isolate and discuss certain elements of the invention process. "It is becoming apparent," Richard Young has observed, "that as new and significant methods of invention emerge, we need to develop a more adequate terminology which distinguishes various arts or methods of invention from *the* art of invention, that is, the members from the class."[5]

Up to this point I have described two types of relationships that help us to map the terrain of rhetorical invention: the contrast between narrow and broad views of rhetorical invention, and the relationship between rhetorical invention and invention in a generic sense. There is yet one other pairing that may usefully be employed to examine past and current conceptions of invention that have prevailed in composition: the contrast between "reflective" and "dynamic" views of invention. A reflective view of invention is based on an assumption that a person finds or discovers something (an idea, thought, fact, or image) either inside the mind or outside in the world, and then simply mirrors or "reflects" it in language. Questioning such an assumption, Linda Flower and John R. Hayes point out that "The myth of discovery implies a method, and this method is based on the premise that hidden stores of insight and ready-made ideas exist, buried in the mind of the writer, waiting only to be 'discovered.'" If ideas are not assumed to be inside the writer, then they are expected to be outside, "to be found in books and data if only the enterprising researcher knows where to look."[6]

This assumption that invention is the discovery or recovery of existing knowledge is evident in many descriptions of processes of writing, from poetry to scientific and technical writing. Novelist Ray Bradbury, for example, says that he gets his ideas from looking in: "All that is most original lies within, waiting for us to summon it forth."[7] In scientific and technical writing, a writer is also assumed to recover existing material, but in this case the writer does not look inside but rather "out there," to ideas and information that have been created prior to discourse. Language is regarded as at best, a vehicle to represent a material object or a process or a scientific abstraction, and at worst, an obstacle or appendage, a necessary evil that conveys some approximation of things or ideas that exist prior to or beyond words. Invention, if it happens at all under these circumstances, is seen as a process of retrieving what is known and getting it to the proper person in the proper way. So in Clarence Andrews' *Technical and Business Writing*, invention is essentially covered in a chapter called "Retrieving Technical Information," with sections on retrieving information from printed matter, from the general public, and from individuals.[8] And in Herman Weisman's *Basic Technical Writing*, report writing is called "Reconstruction of an Investigation"; a report contains "organized, factual, and objective information brought by a person who has experienced or accumulated it to a person or persons who need it, want it, or are entitled to it."[9]

These reflective views of invention in technical writing have a precedent in the work of Francis Bacon, who in the seventeenth century voiced a complaint that the word "invention" was being improperly applied: "for to invent," Bacon wrote, "is to discover that we know not, and not to recover or resummon that which we already know"; in Bacon's view, rhetorical invention was generally (and properly) regarded not as an act of creation but rather of remembering or locating knowledge that people already possessed.[10] To this day the view that invention reflects existing knowledge persists in metaphors and popular mythology about discovery. It is implicit, for instance, in Winston Churchill's statement: "Many men stumble over discoveries, but most of them pick themselves up and walk away."

This interpretation of invention has not gone unchallenged, however, in both classical and modern times. In contemporary science, for instance, Sir Peter Medawar (among others) has attacked a conception of scientific inquiry as an "uncovery" of what is supposed to exist objectively in nature: "Some discoveries *look* as if they were merely a recognition or apprehension of the way nature is; they are lessons learned, as it were, by humbly taking note of what is going on; they have the air of being no more than 'uncoveries' of what was there all the time, waiting to be taken note of." According to Medawar, however, this is a fallacy; "discovery" should be considered an active function: "all such discoveries begin as covert hypotheses," Medawar explains; "that is, as imaginative preconceptions or expectations about the nature of the world and never merely by passive assimilation of the evidence of the senses."[11]

Thus, an alternative view of invention, and indeed of inquiry, emphasizes the role of the rhetor or the investigator in constructing an argument or hypothesis. This is a dynamic view of invention as the creation of something new—new for the individuals or groups who have not previously thought of it, or new in that it has not previously been conceived by anyone at all. The report of the Committee on the Nature of Rhetorical Invention of the Speech Communication Association emphasizes this dynamic view, recommending that the relationship of rhetorical invention and creativity be re-examined, that language be investigated for its inventional role in "transforming world views into argument," and that inquiry be made about the production, as opposed to merely the discovery, of the universal audience for argumentation.[12] In this study, for reasons that will be more fully developed as the argument progresses, my understanding of rhetorical invention is informed by this dynamic view of a process that not only finds but also creates that which is the substance of discourse. Although at times I use phrases such as the "discovery" of new ideas, I resort to such terminology because discovery is a conventional and convenient synonym for invention, not because I want to perpetrate the notion that invention is necessarily a passive act of finding what already exists.

This study, then, brings the work of rhetoricians, philosophers, linguists, and theorists in other fields to bear on the topic of rhetorical invention, broadly and dynamically conceived, to show how it might be better understood if it is viewed as a social act. I will be considering invention as a social act in theory and as it informs the practice and teaching of writing. This first chapter serves to define my understanding of the scope of invention and to provide an overview of the study. Chapter 2 discusses the theoretical problem that is the focus of the study: the inadequacy of a conception prevalent in current composition theory that invention is the act of an atomistic individual who recollects or uncovers ideas from within, all the while remaining apart from a material and social world. I illustrate this Platonic view of invention with examples from the works of several composition theorists. I also suggest several reasons why a Platonic view has gone largely unchallenged, and I assess its strengths and limitations.

Chapter 3 describes what it means to view invention as a social act and discusses precedents for a social view emerging from classical rhetoric. To begin to solve the current problem of inadequate theoretical explanation, Chapter 4 proposes that we supplement a Platonic view with a theoretical framework including what are termed the internal dialogic, collaborative, and collective perspectives on invention. To examine this framework in practice, I include examples drawn from a variety of fields which also serve to illustrate how the study of invention in its generic sense informs our understanding of the social aspects of rhetorical invention.

Chapter 5 makes a theoretical argument about the role of language in a view of invention as a social act: that language is what we use to constitute reality through a dialectic between subject and object, and that this is to be understood as a social process, whether we use language individually or with others. In contemporary Western culture, thought and language are very closely associated as primary modes of cognition and invention. Language thus plays an active role in invention of substance for discourse. Even when the primary agent of invention is an individual, invention is pervasively affected by that individual's relationship to others through language and other socially shared symbol systems. The study concludes with a sixth chapter drawing implications of a view of invention as a social act for writers, researchers, and teachers of writing.

At the present time, when teachers of writing are understandably eager to do carefully controlled empirical research and to translate the results immediately into improved teaching techniques, we should not neglect what can be gained from contemplation of what it is that we are studying. An investigation of theoretical and philosophical perspectives can help us understand the nature of rhetorical invention and the relationship between its individual and social elements. If invention is indeed to be understood as a social act, it is appropriate to explore it by considering the perspectives of major social theorists as well as rhetoricians and philosophers to see how they inform our study of how writers invent. For instance, current composition theories that stress the importance of an internal dialogue during composing—such as Peter Elbow's view of the writer inventing by carrying on an internal dialectic with imagined audiences, or Donald M. Murray's claim that the writer's first audience is an inner "other self" responding to ideas the writer generates—may be tested, questioned, and perhaps supported or more fully developed when considered in relation to analogous theories of internalized others proposed by Sigmund Freud, Harry Stack Sullivan, George Herbert Mead, and Martin Buber.

Writing about current research in rhetoric and composition, Douglas Park states that "our need for new and better techniques counts for little compared to our need for more widely shared wisdom and sophistication," and says that while we may not come to *know* much about the complex process of composing, we can surely hope to *understand* it more fully.[13] I hope that this study will contribute toward an understanding of that important part of the composing process involving the generation of ideas.

2

A Platonic View of
Rhetorical Invention

But how beautiful and legitimate the vivid and emphatic I of Socrates sounds! It is the I of infinite conversation, and the air of conversation is present on all its ways, even before his judges, even in the final hour in prison. This I lived in that relation to man which is embodied in conversation. It believed in the actuality of men and went out toward them. Thus it stood together with them in actuality and is never severed from it. Even solitude cannot spell forsakenness, and when the human world falls silent for him, he hears his *daimonion* say you.

—Martin Buber, *I and Thou*

MARTIN BUBER, IN *I AND THOU*, SPEAKS OF SOCRATES AS ONE who even in solitude embodies an awareness of the other, of Thou; his "I" is an "I of infinite conversation."[1] When the topic of rhetorical invention appears in contemporary composition theory, we are apt to hear much more about the I than about the Thou. Perhaps this disparity has arisen in part because we inherit from the Greeks a paradoxical view of rhetorical invention.

On the one hand, we inherit a view that invention occurs through an inner dialogue with an internalized other; it is an "infinite conversation" similar to what Buber describes as taking place between Socrates' I and his *daimonion*. Such an interchange is essential to

Socratic thought, which comes to us by way of Plato. On the other hand, we find also in Plato a contrasting view of the individual as alone in the search for truth. Invention is seen as a private, asocial act of recollection aimed at uncovering the ultimate truth; invention, in this case, does not require others. "At the outset," says Lawrence Rosenfield, "Plato denied what was for Sophism the very foundation of man's humanness, his impulse to associate with his fellows within the social institution of the *polis*. He claimed that social intercourse necessarily destroys the philosophic act. Hence, solitude became a precondition for thought as he would have it understood."[2]

Western thought has emphasized the latter view of rhetorical invention founded on a belief that truth is accessible by purely individual efforts. More particularly, composition theory and pedagogy in nineteenth and twentieth century America have been founded on a Platonic view of invention, one which assumes that the individual possesses innate knowledge or mental structures that are the chief source of invention. Invention, according to this view, occurs largely through introspective self-examination. Plato maintains that virtues (truth, justice, love) do not exist in the material world, but only in the mind in the shape of ideal forms: perfect prototypes for the natural world, forming an ideal pattern-world of a true, transcendent Reality. Before coming to earth, Plato tells us in the *Phaedrus*, the soul—"Reason's pilot"—visits this realm of ideal forms. Some souls see a great deal of Reality; others see less. But before leaving, all souls drink of the waters of Lethe, which make them forget the truth they have seen.

When these souls are born in us on earth, we try to remember and express what is innate. Those who drank a great deal cannot recollect much at all; others remember more. Some truths are recovered gradually, developing like wings unfolding or plants growing from seeds. Whatever reality we attribute to phenomena in the natural world derives from their sharing to some limited extent in the Reality of ideal forms. Things of the natural world serve as reminders of that realm. The process of reasoning, Socrates tells Phaedrus, is "a remembering of what our soul once saw as it made its journey with a god, looking down upon what we now assert to be real and gazing upwards at what is Reality itself."[3] Thus, individuals come to know not by creating something new but by recollecting.

Invention that proceeds from this perspective is a private activity carried out through introspection and directed by an innate mechanism. This view assumes that an individual possesses knowledge or the structure or mechanism to generate it and that the goal of invention is to express these innate materials, projecting them onto the outside world. Invention is the unfolding of the individual's ideas, feelings, personality, patterns, or voice, all of which are seen as existing independently of others. Standards for judging what is invented do not exist objectively in the external world, nor are they arrived at by consensus. The standard is the abstract ideal of Reality. Just how closely one's expression approximates that ideal is to be decided by the individual, who looks to an internal locus of evaluation.

In using the term "Platonic" for this individualistic view of invention, I must stress that I see this view as based on one enduring and significant interpretation of Plato, not necessarily *the* correct and complete reading of his work.[4] In fact, this interpretive tradition overlooks the Socratic dialogue that I mentioned earlier. Here I am speaking, however, not only of what Plato said, but of what has been *made* of what Plato said. The persisting emphasis in Western thought on the concept of individual apprehension of truth— a concept traditionally credited to Plato—may be to a large degree responsible for a longstanding view of invention as radically individualistic.

In nineteenth century America, for example, Ralph Waldo Emerson's essays on the cultivation of thought and genius conveyed an essentially Platonic view of invention. "Doubt not, O poet, but persist," Emerson exhorts the poet who hopes for genius; "Say 'It is in me, and shall out.'"[5] One of the epigraphs to "Self Reliance" is the Latin saying, *Ne te quaesiveris extra*, meaning "Do not search outside yourself."[6] This emphasis on a self-sufficient inventor persists to the present day, both in popular images of the writer and in classroom practices of teaching writing. Our standard images of writers reflect their solitary modes: the poet in the garret, the novelist in the cabin at the writers' colony, the scholar alone in the library carrel.

In the composition classroom, we as teachers make inquiry a private matter. We give assignments to individuals and look for evidence of invention in a text that is "owned by" an individual. Our students naturally enough come to assume that invention is an episode that is finished when a paper ends—when it receives a grade. When we suggest methods students might use to generate ideas for writing—using the *topoi* or tagmemics or freewriting, for instance—we (and they) assume that these methods are to be used by individuals. Even when students are allowed to brainstorm ideas together or act as peer evaluators in group discussions, the implicit assumption is that others are there primarily to assist the individual. The text that results is usually seen not as a social invention by collaborators but as the property of the person whose name appears at the top of the page. Students who dare to ask if they can actually compose something together are surprised if permission is granted.

Thus, the structure of assignments, courses, and methods of evaluation reflects the tacit assumption that invention is the private, asocial act of a writer for the purpose of producing a text. "Think for yourself," we say, as others said to us; and in so doing, we imply that thinking *for* yourself means thinking *by* yourself. We say this in hopes of attaining laudable goals: increasing a student's self-reliance, encouraging self-expression, rewarding individual effort. With this individualistic emphasis, however, the "self" seems to be an atomistic self rather than an evolving construct that is inevitably social even as it is individual. This atomistic "I" differs considerably from Buber's "I of infinite conversation," which is an I that exists, even in solitude, in constant relation to Thou.

Platonic Invention and Recent Composition Theory

Not only does a Platonic view of rhetorical invention underlie popular images and classroom teaching practices, but it is also evident in the work of recent composition theorists, even those whose views of writing-as-process are regarded as replacing what has been called the current-traditional paradigm. In fact, the persistence of a Platonic view suggests that basic assumptions have perhaps not changed to the extent that a paradigm shift may be said to have taken place. Platonic assumptions are present, for example, in the early theoretical work of Frank D'Angelo as well as in the view of invention (or prewriting) proposed by D. Gordon Rohman and Albert Wlecke. While these views differ in many respects, both imply that invention can be removed from social and material and political concerns;[7] that invention moves from the inside out; and that invention is a process occurring within an introspective, isolated writer. To invent, D'Angelo says, you "reach into the recesses of your mind, to spin out of yourself a thread of thought that will develop into an orderly web."[8] Individuals are thought to possess innate cognitive categories, analogous to the *topoi*, which they project onto the world: "To invent is to extend a system which is already present in the mind."[9]

For Rohman and Wlecke, too, invention moves from the inside out, from writer to world. The writer, they say, seeks a perspective that corresponds to "his own sense of the way things are; and this sense can be discovered only through introspection."[10] The writer's aim is to uncover inner potential, using as techniques freewriting, meditation, and analogy. Much like the Platonic soul on its earthly journey, trying to recollect the Reality it once knew, writers engaged in prewriting "set out in apparent ignorance of what it is that they are groping for; yet they recognize it when they find it" (Rohman and Wlecke, p. 14).

A number of composition articles and textbooks—particularly those concerned with writing as self-expression—depict invention through the metaphor of a seed: an entity that develops according to its inner plan, generating its growth apart from the influence of others, unfolding like the wings of the soul in Plato's metaphor. Such metaphors stress the notion of an autonomous inventor who expresses what is innate. The writer, Rohman and Wlecke say, must "discover that single compelling insight, that 'seed-idea,' that organizing concept which will then 'grow into' language, be realized in the extended sentences and paragraphs of a developing essay" (p. 58). "The seed," D'Angelo notes, "is like the gestalt in the process of invention. It contains within itself everything necessary for a mature development."[11] A primary technique advocated by Gabriele Rico in a book on "natural writing" is the use of a nucleus word as a stimulus for additional associations; a nucleus, Rico says, is "the seed that contains all potential growth."[12] And in *Composition for Personal Growth* by Simon, Hawley, and Britton, the authors complain that education has stunted the growth of the seed in the writer: "This [the writer] is the maturing plant robbed of the full realization of the potentialities which were promised in the seed."[13]

Echoes of Rousseau and Wordsworth are evident in these views of invention. The social and material world, especially as manifested in the educational system, is thought to prevent us from developing what we naturally possess as children. "When we were little we had no difficulty sounding the way we felt," Peter Elbow says; "thus most little children speak and write with real voice."[14] For Elbow, what we try to regain is "real voice"; for Ken Macrorie, it is "truth";[15] for Gabriele Rico, it is "expressive power" and "authenticity" (p. 16). Truly the child here is father to the man. Our goal as writers is to *release* what lies within: writing as "truthtelling" is, for Macrorie, "the great releaser";[16] to write the "natural way," according to the subtitle of Rico's book, you use "right brain techniques to release your expressive powers."

As James Berlin has pointed out in discussing his view of Neo-Platonic rhetoric (which bears certain similarities to what I here call Platonic invention), composition theorists such as the ones I have mentioned do not necessarily believe or deny that writers arrive at a certain truth or a transcendent Reality.[17] It is not that writers must aim to recreate the ideal forms in discourse (which is finally, for Plato, impossible anyway). What is important is the theorists' assumption that writers are trying to express a private sense of what is real for them. This private sense of reality can be known and tested only by looking inward, not by interacting with a material or social world which, to Plato, is illusory and unstable. As a means of invention, then, the outward gaze is not to be trusted.

Why Composition Favors a Platonic View of Invention

Why has this view of rhetorical invention—as the solitary act of an atomistic writer who aims to produce a text—prevailed in composition in America? No doubt because it is compatible with certain assumptions characteristic to Western capitalistic societies in general and academia in particular. Of the many possible explanations for the persistence of a Platonic view, I will note three major ones: the influence of literary studies on composition; the persistence of the romantic myth of the inspired writer; and the widespread effects of capitalism and individualism.

The Influence of Literary Studies

Many of us who teach writing come to it by way of a background in literature and literary theory. English departments in American colleges and universities have their own ways of reinforcing the prevailing cultural emphasis on the individual as opposed to the social collective. English professors have tended to be more interested in an individual person or character than in a group or a social class; more interested in a text than in its relationship to social context; and more interested in the individual, concrete detail than in abstraction and generalization. This preference for the individual unit is seen, for example, in E. B. White's advice, widely regarded as sound: "Don't write about Man, write about a man."[18] Along these lines, Alfred Kazin has stressed that "Literature is the study of individual facts."[19] Terry Eagleton criticizes literary theory because it "assumes, in the main, that at the centre of the world is the contemplative individual self, bowed over its book, striving to gain touch with experience, truth, reality, history, or tradition."[20]

There are, of course, notable exceptions to this general tendency. There have been social histories and biographies that place writers' works in a social context. In recent years, for instance, Nicholas Delbanco's *Group Portrait* shows the relationships among five major writers who lived south of London in 1900, and Noel Riley Fitch's *Sylvia Beach and the Lost Generation* chronicles the fruitful associations of writers, editors, and publishers evolving around Beach's Shakespeare and Company book shop in Paris in the 1920s.[21] Another important exception is the attempt of structuralists to study literature as part of a system. Recent literary critics and philosophers question the individuality and isolation of the author and the text. Roland Barthes, for instance, prefers "to amputate literature from the individual" by regarding authors as "participants in an institutional activity that transcends their individuality."[22]

Yet many of us now teaching writing learned our trade not from teachers who espoused these current literary theories, but from those who were profoundly influenced by New Criticism. With its claim that an individual text is autonomous and self-contained, New Criticism makes it possible to study a text without knowing facts about the author's life, the author's intentions, or the social climate in which the work was composed. The New Critical legacy has accustomed a number of us to looking at individual details or characters, created by an individual author, and occurring in a self-contained text.

It is no wonder that when we turn from literature to composition, we continue to regard both texts and writers as subjects to be studied apart from a social sphere. "The typical English teacher in composition," James Kinneavy has written, "like the traditional English teacher in interpretation of literature, is a true-blue believer in the autonomy of text": "The freshman English theme as it is usually taught is most frequently written without an explicit aim, takes no particular view of its subject matter, is oriented to no particular medium, and is preferably done with no serious thought or preparation. In other words, it is aimless, modeless, mediumless, and unprepared."[23] While the situation is no longer as dire as when Kinneavy made his point, many of us have indeed read "autonomous" themes (and perhaps written them ourselves in English 101) in which the writer and the writing seem to be asocial, and invention appears to occur in a vacuum. This happens at least in part, Kinneavy suggests, because teachers of writing at times rely on methods and assumptions that have been influenced by New Criticism.

Romantic Tradition: The Inspired Writer

For many of us who come to composition by way of literature, the writer's process of creating ideas continues to be imbued with an aura of mystery. Composition researchers who attempt to study writing in quantifiable, empirical studies with results reported in decimal points and standard deviations are frequently met with considerable suspicion. Writing, or more particularly invention, seems much more mysterious than that, and much less certifiable, to those who, consciously or unconsciously, have been guided by romantic views of the writer. Romanticism holds that the writer is inspired from within, as Coleridge claims to have written "Kubla Khan" in a trance, or as Wordsworth made poems that were a "spontaneous overflow of emotion recollected in tranquillity." In the romantic tradition, the inspired writer is apart from others and wants to keep it that way, either to prevent himself and his creations from being corrupted by society, or to maintain a necessary madness (in the style of Poe) that is thought to be, at least in part, the source of art. The processes of inventing and writing become finally inscrutable.

This romantic view of composing is clearly compatible with a Platonic view of invention with its accent on the isolated writer seeking inspiration within. Romantic individualism was particularly evident in the late sixties' emphasis on self-expression, epitomized in the battles of the intuitively good flower child from the country, straight from Rousseau, against the contaminated urban forces of organized bureaucracy. Writing as self-expression was given a boost by this kind of romantic rebellion; books and workshops on journal-writing as therapy have continued to be popular over the past fifteen years.[24] A current resurgence of romanticism, one which reinforces a Platonic view of invention, may be surfacing in the works of composition teachers who emphasize the roles played in writing by the left and right hemispheres of the brain. For example, the previously mentioned textbook by Gabriele Rico, titled *Writing the Natural Way: Using Right-Brain Techniques to Release Your Expressive Powers*, asserts that the left brain, identified with language, rationality, and logic, is developed in Western educational systems, while the intuitive functions of the right brain are virtually ignored. Since writing "the natural way," according to Rico, is lost during education, one must regain the child-like state by tapping the resources latent in the right brain. As a writer, Rico maintains, you must learn "to rekindle your creative expressive powers that began when you first learned to speak—in the uninhibited delight you had in using words long before formal rules and painful criticism blocked your natural drive for self-expression" (p. 16).

While it remains to be seen how composition will benefit from right brain/left brain theory or research, at present this dichotomy functions as a metaphor for a familiar polarity. Pitting the repressed right brain against the dominant left in the composing process may be yet another version—this time internalized in the brain and scientized—of the battle of the flower child versus the bureaucracy or the noble savage versus society. In classical times, to talk about invention, the philosopher looked within the soul and hoped to watch its wings unfold; in a technological era, the neurophysiologist looks inside the brain and hopes to measure electrochemical activity at the synapses. Both the literary scholar and the composition teacher with literary roots will likely be more at home with the image of the solitary poet in the garret or with Plato's metaphor of the soul's unfolding wings than with the scientist's measurements of discharges at synapses. Oddly enough, however, these metaphors, including the metaphorical discharges at synapses, share striking commonalities:

each is consistent with a Platonic view that a writer invents alone, by cultivating what is already within.

Capitalism, Individualism, and Invention

One would expect the predominant ideology of a society and its received views about the nature of human thought to affect and reinforce one another. Thus it is not surprising that the work of Soviet psychologists such as L. S. Vygotsky and A. R. Luria stresses a reciprocal relationship between social activity and individual cognition, accomplished by language. Vygotsky's research investigates and supports the premise that thought as inner speech derives from outer, social speech.[25] Luria's *Cognitive Development: Its Cultural and Social Foundations* explains that Soviet psychology rejects the idea that consciousness represents an "intrinsic property of mental life" present in each person's mental state, and operating independently from historical developments. Luria bases his study on the assumption that consciousness is not something given in advance but is shaped by social activity and used to restructure conditions as well as to adapt to them. His experiments with Russian peasants confirmed his hypothesis that an individual's mental processes and self-perception depend on, and change with, social history and social practices such as education and the organization of labor.[26]

Just as Vygotsky and Luria were likely swayed by Soviet ideology to view consciousness as a socially influenced entity, so are we in America influenced by our ideology of capitalism joined with individualism to view invention in both its rhetorical and generic senses as an individual phenomenon. Our widespread "Columbus complex"—the compulsion to credit each discovery to an individual inventor—was no doubt promoted by the development of the printing press. As Elizabeth Eisenstein points out in *The Printing Press as an Agent of Change*, print made it easier to identify an inventive act with one individual as distinguished from others. Before the printing press, it was difficult not only to distinguish what was merely recovered or repeated from what was truly new, but also to identify the author of a given idea or tale. Stories were spread orally; a set text was seldom available; and one could not know with certainty how much one narrator embellished the "original" tale of another. Many works were simply credited to *anon.*[27]

Medieval lack of specificity about authorship may have had its reasons, Daniel Boorstin has noted, since the preservation of dogma was valued more than innovation, and the monks who served as scribes may thus have been reluctant to take the blame or credit for writing an original text. Current conventions of attribution, such as the use of quotation marks and bylines, did not exist. Quotation marks were not in use until the fifteenth century, so it was difficult to indicate exactly which words were borrowed from others. Names were not always attached to manuscripts, and even when they were, they did not establish what we have come think of as authorship. For instance, the title "Sermones Bonaventurae" on a medieval manuscript from a Franciscan monastery might mean, Boorstin explains, that the sermons were either composed, preached, collected, copied, or owned by a monk named Bonaventura.[28]

On the one hand, the creation of print may be said to have aided the social process of invention since, as Eisenstein explains, print made works more accessible and thus made it possible for people to identify and build on each others' ideas and accomplishments. On the other hand, however, once print made it possible for texts to be established and identified with a certain author, writing could be regarded as the property of an individual person. With printing, Eisenstein notes, came laws regarding patents and copyrights, along with the desire to distinguish ideas and works that were privately owned from those in the public domain.[29] Once authorship could be identified and preserved, the concept became so widely accepted, particularly in capitalistic systems, that its value has rarely been questioned. By the same token, inventional theory based on the assumption that individuals develop their own ideas from within and then claim ownership for what they invent (through patent or copyright or simply a name on a term paper) is certainly in line with the aims of Western capitalistic societies, in which ideas and discoveries, like nearly everything else, become property owned by individuals, able to be bought and sold.[30]

In America, the fusion of capitalism, individualism, and patriarchal assumptions has further reinforced a Platonic view of invention in both its rhetorical and generic realms. In discussing prevalent views of creativity in America, Harold Lasswell has criticized the tendency to look exclusively to the individual rather than to social elements:

In our individualistic tradition it is natural to look for the creative individual: the Benthams in politics, the Adam Smiths in economics, the Akhenatons in ethics and religion, the da Vincis in prodigality of skilled expression, the Galileos in the march of human enlightenment, the Great Emancipators in the history of respect for human dignity and the overcoming of caste, the Pasteurs in the overcoming of disease, the Rousseaus in the creation of styles in intimacy of expression.[31]

John W. Gardner, too, notes the tendency to emphasize the role of a single discoverer, even though new ideas often come about by means of cumulative minor changes, many of which are anonymous. "Our dramatic sense (or our superficiality)," Gardner says, "leads us to seek out 'the man who started it all' and to heap on his shoulders the whole credit for a prolonged, diffuse, and infinitely complex process."[32] Similarly, John R. Pierce has stated that "An innovation is no less legitimate for having two fathers, but it is troublesome for the historian."[33]

While neither Lasswell, Gardner, nor Pierce comments on the issue of gender, their emphasis on the masculine—whether it be through the choice of men as examples of innovators or the use of words such as "man" and "father"—is typical of much of the published history of creative ideas, which has until quite recently focused on men rather than women. Even when the "mothers" of invention are acknowledged, the individualistic emphasis may remain. For instance, as Dale Spender explains, the traditional identification of the beginning of the women's movement with Mary Wollstonecraft made Wollstonecraft seem a solitary and aberrant figure. When Spender began to question what she terms a "patriarchal" portrayal of history—the identification of a radically new idea as the singular act of a solitary individual—her research uncovered evidence of many other women protestors, both predecessors and contemporaries of Wollstonecraft, women whom she would otherwise have missed.[34] In effect, then, it seems likely that if we look through patriarchal spectacles to see how new ideas have developed, we will tend to find the solitary agent of invention whom we seek, even as we overlook the often necessary others.

A further explanation of how patriarchal assumptions affect the traditional view of invention may be derived from the research of psychologist Carol Gilligan. In studying the moral reasoning and development of males and females, Gilligan found that men tend to make moral decisions based on abstract principles, whereas women make such decisions based on the ways people are connected to each other and the consequences of actions on their relationships. These differences, Gilligan maintains, arise from the tendency of men to assume that they are autonomous, and the contrasting tendency of women to assume that they are defined in part by their connections with others. While recognizing that these are two distinct ways of viewing the self in relation to others, Gilligan suggests that one need not necessarily be regarded as superior to the other. She notes, however, that the female approach accenting social relationships has been widely misunderstood and devalued, while the male approach accenting autonomy has been considered the "correct" one.[35] The persistence of such an ideal of individual autonomy in male-centered, capitalistic culture further explains why a Platonic view of invention, which stresses the writer as an isolated unit apart from material and social forces, has been widely accepted.

In summary, then, there are enduring intellectual and cultural traditions that support a Platonic view of invention: traditions in literary studies emphasizing the individual unit as a focus of study; romantic notions of the isolated creator, inspired from within; and a strong regard for individualism in capitalistic, patriarchal societies. The Platonic view fits smoothly as well with other prevalent (though not necessarily sacrosanct) traditions in Western thought: the Cartesian ego, the cognitive "mind," and the psychoanalytic concentration on the psyche of the individual. Considering the combined force of these elements, all of which are compatible with a view of invention as the act of an atomistic individual, it is not surprising that such a view has received few serious challenges as an adequate explanation of invention.

Strengths and Limitations of a Platonic View

Theories of invention based on Platonic assumptions have made a clear contribution to our developing understanding of invention and the composing process. The articulation of such theories, together with a revival of classical rhetoric that acknowledges the importance of invention, has directed our attention to rhetorical invention, thus saving it from a long period of neglect. Furthermore, theories based on a Platonic view have given rise to inventional methods—the use of analogy, freewriting, and clustering—that often help writers to break through conventional stereotypes of perception and expression, reassuring them that they do have many possibilities and resources within. The emphasis that a Platonic view places on self-analysis and reflection may encourage individuals to use writing to explore issues that are of personal significance.

As a primary way of explaining the process of rhetorical invention, however, a Platonic view alone is inadequate, chiefly because it promotes an oversimplified view of what an individual is and because it is not sufficiently comprehensive to account for what happens when writers invent. What follows is a summary of its key limitations.

A Platonic view of invention leads us to favor individualistic approaches to research and to neglect studies of writers in social contexts. Historically, invention has been neglected as a subject of inquiry because it has been thought of as a private and personal activity. How, after all, should we study an act that is thought to be hidden, mysterious, and inaccessible to many research methodologies? When invention *has* been studied, the method has generally been to investigate the individual person as an isolated unit in the episodic act of composing a single text. Typically the researcher has relied on a writer's testimony about the invention process, or studies of a writer's text, or, more recently, analysis of protocols in which the writer says aloud what she is thinking as she composes. Influences on invention that come from interpersonal transactions or from forces originating in social collectives have received relatively little attention.

The field of composition studies has been described by Patricia Bizzell as including two theoretical camps: those who see writing as primarily "inner-directed," concentrating on the processes of cognition and language acquisition as they exist universally, "prior to social influence"; and those who stress the "outer-directed" nature of writing, concentrating on the "social processes whereby language-learning and thinking capacities are shaped and used in particular communities."[36] Bizzell argues that inner-directed theory can be complemented and enlarged by outer-directed views: "Composition

studies should focus on practice within interpretive communities—
exactly how discourse communities work in the world and how they
are transmitted."[37] Research and scholarship based on a view of invention as a social act—rather than an "inner-directed" act of a solitary writer whose invention is thought to be based on innate univer-
sals—would, I think, square with the outer-directed studies which
Bizzell is advocating.

Even in outer-directed studies of social processes, individuals may
still remain the focus of study as primary agents of invention. I will
maintain, however (particularly in chapter 5, which concerns the
role of language in invention), that invention is best understood as a
social act even when its agent is an individual. Quite often, moreover, agency is more appropriately attributed to two or more people
who collaborate to create something new. Business proposals, technical documentation, reports of scientific research, contracts,
treaties, and political platforms—all are typically the invention of
more than one person. The many types of co- and group-authorship
and mutual influence are only beginning to be studied systemati-
cally,[38] and the delay in such work is no doubt due in large part to
the prevalence of a Platonic view of invention, which has focused
attention on the individual writer and his text.

A Platonic view depicts invention as a closed, one-way system. A
Platonic view assumes that an individual finds and expresses latent
thoughts (or an inner voice or authentic self) by means of introspection. While common sense tells us that invention does occur
through introspection, it is more usefully regarded as a special kind
of introspection involving an exchange between the individual and
the socioculture. In a comprehensive book on creativity, Silvano
Arieti analyzes the interrelationships of society, culture, and the individual. He concludes that some societies are "creativogenic," en-
hancing creativity in individuals, while others are restrictive, inhibiting the growth of creativity.

Creativity, according to Arieti, occurs within the psyche of individuals, but it occurs as part of an open system requiring material
from the external world, and it is subject to change because of sociocultural influences. Creativity results from the partnership of a potentially creative person and a creativogenic society and culture. It
is not sufficient to study either the individual or the society, or to try
to enhance creativity in one but not the other. New ideas are in-

vented when cultural elements interact and are synthesized in an individual psyche. In certain creative individuals, Arieti argues, a match or a meshing occurs of characteristics of the individual with the characteristics made available by the socioculture at a given time and place. The "magic synthesis" that these individuals achieve creates something new that in turn goes into the socioculture, which may itself change as a result.[39]

A seed metaphor does not accurately represent this process, Arieti claims. Whereas one knows that an acorn, given proper conditions, must become an oak and nothing else, one does not know of such a certain outcome for an individual who has potential for creativity. The acorn lives in a closed system, while the creative individual lives in an open system. Rain does not change in response to the acorn's growth, but culture may change in response to an individual's creation, and the individual, too, may change as a result of interaction with her sociocultural environment.

A Platonic view of invention presupposes a closed system, with the individual's invention developing like a seed. This view does not allow for the individual's interaction with and response to a world of people and things and symbolic forms; nor does it note how social and cultural features are embedded in each individual; nor does it show how individual and culture are interdependent.

A Platonic view abstracts the writer from society. Like the Marlboro man or the Virginia Slims woman, the writer is portrayed as an individual who is supremely self-reliant. When we promote or tacitly accept this Platonic view, we teach our students more than how to write an essay. In a discussion of theories of pedagogy in contemporary composition, James Berlin notes that teachers of writing teach more than writing *per se*: "in teaching writing we are tacitly teaching a version of reality and the student's place and mode of operation in it" (p. 766). A teaching method based on what Berlin calls "Neo-Platonic Rhetoric" communicates a sense that the writer is "at the center of the rhetorical act" but at the same time is "finally isolated, cut off from community, and left to the lonely business of discovering truth alone" (p. 776).

To succeed in teaching writing, then, it follows that those who assume a Platonic view would teach students to do a better job of "discovering truth alone." In his 1976 book, *English in America*, Richard Ohmann concludes that writing teachers have unfortu-

done just that. Most composition textbooks, Ohmann says, s the uses of writing "in terms of the individual student, abed from society. Mainly, they offer him greater powers of thought or self-discovery than he could otherwise attain"; often the writer's self is assumed to be the source of invention in that the self possesses topics, which are thought to be "inertly there, waiting to be mined" (p. 150). Charles Yarnoff, too, criticizes contemporary theories of invention that conceive of the individual as apart from a material or social realm, investigating an abstract realm of ideas. Such an approach, Yarnoff claims, teaches students that writing has little to do with material reality, and thus trivializes writing; it teaches students to operate solely on the basis of an internal locus of evaluation which is ill-defined, and says nothing about the evaluation of what is invented based on standards from the material or social world (p. 553).

One pays a price for this hidden instruction about the nature of invention. While a Platonic view may encourage individuals to look within and release ideas, it may in some instances be counterproductive, thwarting creative thinking. Group brainstorming, synectics groups, management teams, and team research in science all exist because people are aware that they may have better ideas when they collaborate. If we teach people to stay apart when they invent and to compete with each other for grades or other compensation for their ideas, they may fail to take advantage of the synergy that can arise from social interactions. People may be so inexperienced at inventing together that they cannot stop competing long enough to realize the benefits of collaboration. Furthermore, people who grow accustomed to the idea that invention is supposed to be a solitary act may feel that if they have difficulty inventing in some situations, they have only themselves to blame. Something must be wrong inside them. It seldom occurs to them that the ways they interact with others and with social collectives could have something to do with inventional failures as well as successes.

A Platonic view assumes and promotes the concept of the atomistic self as inventor. This atomistic Western self is, as Wayne Booth sees it, isolated, competitive, and aggressive, though able on occasion to compromise in social-contract style, giving up one "piece" of the self in exchange for someone else's. Booth describes the myths of scientism and irrationalism that evolve from the assumption of the self as an isolated unit. Under scientism, the goal of the self is to find out enough about human nature and nature in general to control both, so one can get what one wants. Under irrationalism, the goal is to discover and define one's self, as opposed to everyone else's self.[40]

In composition, the myth of irrationalism is apparent, for example, in a 1983 advertisement for a textbook called *Writing Your Way*, which says "This book . . . urges you to fill blank paper with the stuff of your world and not someone else's." Am I to assume, then, that I can know "my" world apart from someone else's? Is my world necessarily so separate? Do I define my self and my world in opposition to others? Novelist Margaret Atwood is critical of the emphasis often placed on the writer as an enclosed self. "Readers and critics both are still addicted to the concept of self-expression," Atwood says, "the writer as a kind of spider, spinning out his entire work from within. This view depends on a solipsism, the idea that we are all self-enclosed monads, with an inside and an outside, and that nothing from the outside ever gets in."[41] The myth about writing as the expression of what lies within this "self-enclosed monad" is in part responsible, Atwood claims, for the popular misconception that writing is not serious work. All one must do, it seems, is look within at one's own experience (which is assumed to be within rather than without), and simply let it out.[42] Invention becomes a matter of expressing (from the Latin *ex pressare*, "to press out") one's ego.

Over a century ago, Tocqueville saw this coming. Writing about individualism in democracies, he pointed out that it begins by destroying all public virtues and finally wipes out all the others, too, returning to its original and less genteel state of egoism. The increase of equality in America, Tocqueville predicted, would create a large group of people who would have money and power enough to look out for themselves, but would lack connection with others. "Such folk owe no man anything and hardly expect anything from anybody," Tocqueville wrote, adding this warning: "Each man is thrown back on himself alone," there to be imprisoned in "the solitude of his own heart."[43]

America thus offers the advantage of a certain degree of autonomy along with the disadvantage of a false sense of self-sufficiency that leads to self-absorption. In *The Pursuit of Loneliness: American Culture at the Breaking Point*, Philip Slater argues that Americans secretly desire interdependence and community, even while overtly undermining any such collective yearnings. Technology and free enterprise are used to promote an unrealistic independence, Slater says: "We seek a private house, a private means of transportation, a private garden, a private laundry, self-service stores, and do-it-yourself skills of every kind. An enormous technology seems to have set itself the task of making it unnecessary for one human being ever to ask anything of another in the course of going about his daily business."[44] Increased computerization, Slater points out, also has the effect of making contact with people less necessary. A major goal of invention in contemporary America, then, seems to be to "help" us become more individualistic than ever.

If, on the other hand, we are inclined to reconsider the received Western view of the self as thinker and inventor, what are our alternatives? The answer to that question is well beyond the scope of this book, but there are, in fact, many sources to which we can turn, as anthropologist Clifford Geertz has noted: "The Western conception of the person as a bounded, unique, more or less integrated motivational and cognitve universe, a dynamic center of awareness, emotion, judgment, and action organized into a distinctive whole and set contrastively both against other such wholes and against its social and natural background, is, however incorrigible it may seem to us, a rather peculiar idea within the contexts of the world's cultures."[45] For example, Geertz notes, Morroccans refer to a person not with a unique, fixed name but with a *nisba*, a term that changes to indicate the person's relation to certain social groups or contexts. One would never be called simply "Umar," Geertz explains, but "Umar Al-Buhadiwi" (Umar of the Buhadiwi tribe) or "Umar Al-Sussi" (Umar from the Sus region), or some other label that associates the individual with a religion, occupation, or family. The use of the *nisba*, Geertz claims, suggests that persons are not regarded as "bounded psychic entities detached from their backgrounds and singularly named," but rather as selves that "gain their definition from associative relations they are imported to have with the society that surrounds them. They are contextualized persons."[46]

Geertz is but one of the many theorists in a diversity of fields—anthopology, sociology, philosophy, religion, rhetoric—whose work points toward a reconceptualization of the self as a social entity. Others whose views are suggestive include Martin Buber's view of the I as formed in the relationship with the Thou; Georg Simmel's view of the dialectical relationship between the individual and society; George Herbert Mead's theories of the generation of meaning through social interaction and genesis of the self through social relationships that become internalized as a "generalized other"; Emile Durkheim's analysis of the social collective; and Gregory Bateson's "ecology of mind," conceiving a self "not bounded by skin" but interacting constantly with the environment.[47] Of particular relevance to this study is Wayne Booth's proposal for revising the myths and assumptions concerning the autonomous, isolated individual. Booth prefers to think of the self as a "field of selves":

> What happens, then, if we choose to begin with our knowledge that we are essentially creatures made in symbolic interchange, created in the process of sharing intentions, values, meanings; in fact more like each other than different, more valuable in our commonality than in our idiosyncracies: not, in fact, anything at all when considered separately from our relations? What happens if we think of our selves as essentially participants in a field or process or mode of *being persons together*?[48]

The view that Booth expresses, according to S. Michael Halloran, offers a "beginning of a humanistic rationale" that balances the classical emphasis on the orator, who identified completely with his social role of embodying society, and the contrasting modern emphasis on the autonomous rhetor, concerned not with a social function but with expressing his authentic, private voice.[49] To take Booth's suggestion and regard ourselves as "being persons together" or, by extension, being inventors together, we would indeed have to travel some distance from a Platonic view of invention.

A Platonic view fails to acknowledge that invention is collaborative. While knowledge, as Richard Ohmann has pointed out, is a social product—"the greatest innovator adds only an iota to the structure of ideas he inherits"—a Platonic view of invention reinforces the capitalistic accent on ideas as the creation and property of an individual inventor. Once individuals are credited with owning an idea, they are frequently allowed to apply it as they see fit. This entrepreneurial freedom has had unfortunate consequences, Ohmann notes, in a world in which constantly expanding technological innovations inevitably affect others and in which individuals who "own" an idea have exploited resources that all supposedly share (*English in America*, p. 317).

The individualistic view of rhetorical invention goes hand in hand with conventional ways of acknowledging inventors of material objects, ideas, and texts. We tend to assume that a book with one author listed on the cover has one and the same inventor. But there may have been more than one person pushing the pen, and there were almost certainly others behind the byline: those whose work the author built on or adapted; those whose criticism prompted further invention; and those who created an environment in which that writer could invent. We learn about these hidden enablers in prefaces and acknowledgments, interviews or biographies. These provide hints, and sometimes solid evidence, that invention may be an overtly social act. Here we find evidence, for example, of the "To my wife without whom" syndrome: a man receives ideas from a woman; he claims and receives authorship; she gets mentioned in the preface or dedication, in what comes before the "real" book begins. While this same pattern of behavior could, of course, be used by women to the disadvantage of men, it has historically been the case that, intentionally or not, the contributions of women have more often been the ones overlooked. As Joanna Russ explains, assigning women to "false categories"—that is, allowing their ideas and efforts to be "absorbed into a man's and recategorized as his"—has been a popular way of of suppressing women's creativity; women find that their ideas receive little or no acknowledgment and come to expect that their proper role is to play the supporting part of enabling creativity in others.[50]

An instructive example comes from novelist John Gardner, who has at least, as Tillie Olsen notes in quoting him, been forthright in articulating his opinion, which is more than one can say of many authors whom Olsen calls "leech-writers."[51] Gardner acknowledges his wife's contribution to his fiction, but not to the point of deeming it coauthorship:

> If I have any doubts about what a character would say or what a room would look like, I ask my wife. . . . Perhaps I should have used "John and Joan Gardner" on the titles all along; I may do this in the future. But in modern times such work is regarded as not really art. The notion that art is an individual and unique vision is a very unmedieval and unclassical view. In the Middle Ages it was very common to have several people work on one thing: the thirteenth century Vulgate cycle of Arthurian ro-

mances had hundreds of writers. I feel comfortable with this approach, but I haven't felt comfortable telling people it's what I do. As I get more and more into the medieval mode, I'll probably admit how many writers I have.[52]

Asked if his wife is a collaborator on his books, Gardner replies: "I use a lot of people, Joan in particular. She hasn't actually written any lines, because Joan's too lazy for that. But she's willing to answer questions. The extent of her contribution doesn't quite approach collaboration in the modern sense."[53] *She hasn't actually written any lines*: perhaps the act of writing, then, is what now constitutes "official" collaboration? As Gardner's comments suggest, in contemporary Western culture, answering the writer's questions doesn't seem to count as coauthorship. Nor does describing characters and settings. Reading, conducting interviews, doing research, taking notes, checking facts, adding details, making phone calls, organizing, typing, proofreading, indexing—all of these are tasks for which people are often credited in acknowledgments of books that nevertheless have but one designated author. Words spoken or actions taken seldom count as authorship: what counts is what is fixed and can be pointed to: what is written in a text.

If we take a rhetorical view of the entire process of invention instead of focusing on the production of a text, we may be more inclined to regard talking and acting as part of the process, as surely they should be. In his preface to *The Structure of Scientific Revolutions*, Thomas Kuhn notes how his relationships with others—James B. Conant, Leonard K. Nash, and Stanley Cavell—contributed to the development of ideas. Cavell's contribution was his ability to understand what could not yet be clearly articulated: "He is the only person," Kuhn says, "with whom I have ever been able to express my ideas in incomplete sentences."[54] This is a type of collaboration that surpasses the written and the spoken word. A Platonic view of invention does not, however, recognize its significance.

While co- and group-authorship have not traditionally been acknowledged in English classrooms where, as Gardner says, a collaborative fiction "is regarded as not really art," collaborative invention is more acceptable in other disciplines such as science and business, where groups of people more often work together to generate ideas. A view of invention that acknowledges its social aspects may be particularly useful to those who aim to promote the teaching of writing across the curriculum. The predominance of a Platonic view is likely responsible for some of the antagonism that arises between teachers in English departments and those in other fields over how and why writing should be taught. Faculty in other disciplines often assume that English teachers are interested primarily in having students "express themselves," whereas other teachers have something quite different in mind. Their suspicion of English teachers, while it may be exacerbated by an oversimplified view of a supposed dichotomy between "expressive" and "communicative" writing, nonetheless reveals their assumption that what I have described as a Platonic view prevails among the English faculty. Allowing a Platonic view to assume such prominence is thus subversive to the aims of those both in and out of English departments who wish to promote writing across the curriculum.

In summary, then, a Platonic view of rhetorical invention has been valuable in that it has helped bring recognition to the role of invention as an integral part of the composing process, and it has influenced writers positively by encouraging reflection and reassuring them that they do have important resources within. At the same time, it limits our understanding of invention in several important ways: it leads us to study the individual inventor apart from sociocultural contexts; it depicts invention as a closed, one-way system, and the inventor as an atomistic unit, abstracted from society; and it fails to acknowledge that invention is often a collaborative process. In the rest of this study I will explore how these limitations may be overcome, and invention more comprehensively understood, by adopting a social perspective.

3

Invention as
a Social Act

So far I have described a Platonic view of rhetorical invention, given examples of its use in composition theory, said why such a view has predominated, and explored its strengths and limitations. I have, in effect, shown what a social perspective on invention is *not*. Now let's see what it is.

Invention, conceived broadly as the process of actively creating as well as finding what comes to be known and said in the discourse of any discipline, is, I think, best understood as occurring when individuals interact dialectically with socioculture in a distinctive way to generate something. In this chapter I will describe what I mean by viewing invention as *social*, as *dialectical*, and as an *act*. To place this view in a context, I will briefly consider both contemporary and classical theoretical approaches with which it is compatible.

Social Aspects of Invention

Taking as a starting point Max Weber's definition of "social" as that which is oriented to take into account the behavior of others,[1] one can regard invention as social in various ways. The following summary highlights several significant social aspects of invention, each of which is explored in greater detail elsewhere in this study.

1. The inventing "self" is socially influenced, even socially constituted, according to a variety of theorists such as George Herbert Mead, Martin Buber, Clifford Geertz, and Wayne Booth. With this

perspective, invention may be seen as social even when its agent is a single individual.

2. One invents with language or with other symbol systems, which are socially created and shared by members of discourse communities. The important role that language in particular plays in invention provides another rationale for regarding invention as social even when its agent is an individual, a point to be explored more fully in chapter 5.

3. Invention builds on a foundation of knowledge accumulated from previous generations, knowledge that constitutes a social legacy of ideas, forms, and ways of thinking. "Contrary to Sisyphus," Silvano Arieti points out, "the creative man does not start from the foot of the mountain again, but from where other people have left off."[2] Each creative act is given to another generation of thinkers who may dismiss, confirm, or build on it.

4. Invention may be enabled by an internal dialogue with an imagined other or a construct of audience that supplies premises or structures of belief guiding the inventor. Writing about various perceptions of audience in composition theory and pedagogy, Lisa Ede and Andrea Lunsford stress the importance of recognizing an "internal dialogue, through which writers analyze inventional problems and conceptualize patterns of discourse."[3] This inner dialogue, the existence of which is generally assumed by researchers who rely on think-aloud protocols, is thought by Vygotsky and others to be a process one learns through social interactions that subsequently become internalized.

5. Writers often invent by involving other people: as editors and evaluators whose comments aid further invention; as "resonators" who nourish and sustain the inventor as well as the invention; as collaborators who interact to create new ideas; and as opponents or devil's advocates who provide challenges and alternate perspectives to work against. To create certain kinds of discourses such as contracts or treaties, two or more rhetors (often in adversarial positions) must collaborate in order to invent.

6. Invention is powerfully influenced by social collectives, such as institutions, bureaucracies, governments, and "invisible colleges" of academic disciplinary communities. These collectives, to be discussed more fully in the next chapter, serve to transmit expectations and prohibitions, encouraging or discouraging certain ideas, areas of

investigation, methods of inquiry, types of evidence, and rhetorical forms.

7. The reception, evaluation, and use of what is invented depend to a great extent on social context. Writing in the 1930s about the discovery process in science, Ludwik Fleck noted that it is essential to consider the influence of social conditions and community, even in the case of apparently independent, or personal, exploits. "Such scientific exploits," Fleck explains, "can prevail only if they have a seminal effect by being performed at a time when the social conditions are right."[4]

Invention as a Dialectical Process

Invention is a *dialectical process* in that the inventing individual(s) and the socioculture are co-existing and mutually defining. Their relationship is analogous to the relationship between Martin Buber's I and Thou (You): "I require a You to become; becoming I, I say You."[5] New ideas are created by this dialectical partnership. Individual human agents always act in the context of their interconnections with others, as John Dewey has told us: "Individuals still do the thinking, desiring, and purposing, but *what* they think of is the consequence of their behavior upon that of others and that of others upon themselves."[6] What is unique about the individual inventor is his or her particular way of interacting with others and with socioculture—as Dewey puts it, "a *distinctive* way of behaving in conjunction with and *connection* with other distinctive ways of acting, not a self-enclosed way of acting, independent of everything else" (p. 188).

Contrary to this dialectical view, much that has been said in the past about the sources of invention and creativity has concentrated on either the individual *or* the socioculture. As we have seen in the previous discussion of a Platonic view of rhetorical invention, the atomistic individual has frequently been regarded as the primary agent of invention and thus the proper focus of study. The literature of creativity in a variety of fields is replete with studies that attempt to determine what traits creative individuals possess. Occasionally (though less often) one finds studies based on the opposite assumption: that society or culture is the instigator of new ideas, which are manifested through an individual when the time is ripe for the ideas to be thought. Along these lines, Alfred Kroeber and Charles Edward Gray both consider culture to be the primary force of creativity. For Kroeber, individual personalities are "inevitable mechanisms or measures of cultural expression"; for Gray, creative individuals are "an index of the growth of their cultures" (Kroeber and Gray, quoted by Arieti, p. 298).

In composition, stressing the role of culture over that of the individual would have the advantage of being refreshingly different, and it certainly would make one look at invention in a new way. It would finally be unsatisfying, however, for in reducing the role of the individual to that of a mere vehicle, it would still fail to explain why one individual rather than another would be apt to think of a new idea. Why, Silvano Arieti asks, when conditions seem "right" in a culture for a discovery to be made, does the synthesis that prompts the discovery take place in only a small percentage of people? And why is this accomplished by one person or group rather than another (p. 302)?

Arieti's answer to these questions, which I take to be a reasonable hypothesis, is that the characteristics of certain people mesh with characteristics made available by their socioculture at a given time and place. The "magic synthesis" or invention made by these individuals goes back into the culture, which may itself change as a result (pp. 304–11). A culture cannot "think" ideas without the synthesis made possible by individuals who interact with culture in certain ways, nor can individuals create ideas in a vacuum removed from society and culture.

Even if we are persuaded that, as this study argues, social elements are indeed inextricably involved in invention, it will still be tempting to think of "individual" and "social" as mutually exclusive oppositions or to give priority to one over the other. We may, for example, wonder about questions such as these: When invention occurs, what exactly is contributed by social elements, and what by the individual? Does an individual first think of an idea—in a pure, "asocial" state—and then censor or change or express it only after subjecting it to socially determined standards? Is the individual inventor the primary actor in a scene in which the social context serves merely as a backdrop? Or is the social collective the principal agent of invention?

Such questions, intriguing though they may seem, and aimed

understandably at resolving problems of causality, are finally not the most fruitful ones to ask. Framed in terms of unhelpful oppositions, they imply that "individual" and "social" can be neatly separated, and that one can be said to cause the other. What I am suggesting, however, is that they be regarded as dialectically connected, always codefining and interdependent. A change in the individual influences social dimensions, which in turn influence the individual. Since every act may cause a reaction that in turn prompts another adjustment or action, it is impossible to say which is first, or which predominates.[7]

At a certain point, one might suppose, there could have been an individual—an atom, an Adam, a wild boy of Aveyron—without a socioculture. But for all practical purposes, the two have, since that theoretically "pure" moment of aloneness, been inextricably wound together. To borrow Clifford Geertz's metaphor of the onion, one cannot peel away the social to get at the individual; they are the same entity. Or as Arieti puts it, "man without culture would be limited to the dark core of *I*. He would be entirely a biological entity, not a sociological entity as we know him" (p. 307).

So the antithesis that these oppositions suggest is misleading, which is what Dewey told us fifty years ago: "both words, individual and social, are hopelessly ambiguous, and the ambiguity will never cease as long as we think in terms of an antithesis" (p. 186). Common sense, Dewey notes, does direct our attention toward that which seems to be spatially separate, which "moves and acts as a unitary thing," leading us to consider that as the "individual" (p. 187). Yet that which appears to be a separate unit is seldom so; even the seemingly "individual" tree must live in soil and be fed by water, air, and light, which are in turn the by-products of processes of other living things. One should be wary, Dewey notes, of defining the individual being as a unit that operates in a separate sphere, a kind of "residual individual who is not a member of any association at all" (p. 191). Perhaps the isolated, atomistic inventor, like the asocial individual, is ultimately a supreme fiction.

Invention as an Act

Up to this point, then, we have considered ways in which invention may be seen as social and as a dialectical process involving individuals and socioculture. In adopting a social perspective on rhetorical invention, it is furthermore desirable to view invention as an act: first, an act that is generally initiated by an inventor (or rhetor) and brought to completion by an audience; and second, an act that involves symbolic activities such as speaking or writing and often extends over time through a series of social transactions and texts.

Inventor and Audience

To develop the first point—that invention is enacted by inventor and audience—I rely on Hannah Arendt's discussion of "action," which in turn derives from the Greek and Latin double meaning of the word. Action, Arendt says, was previously regarded as having two parts: "the beginning made by a single person and the achievement in which many join by 'bearing' and 'finishing' the enterprise, by seeing it through."[8] The word has since lost this double meaning, according to Arendt, with action being split into the role of giving commands and the role of executing them. The one who initiates commands now appears to be isolated from others. We may regard such a person as independent and powerful in her apparent isolation, but in fact, Arendt insists, such a person is not isolated at all; the potential for power requires the presence of others, and the achievement of action requires that others execute and thus complete the action.

To understand rhetorical invention, it is useful to restore this double meaning of "action" and think of the act of invention as having two parts: the initiation of the inventive act and the reception or execution of it. The inventor thus requires the presence of the other. This "other" may at times be another part of the rhetor herself—an internalized construct that she makes from social experience—or it may be a perceived audience of actual others. It may be a collaborator with whom one invents or a reader whose participation in constructing a text "finishes" the enterprise.

Viewing invention as a collaborative act on the part of writer and reader may seem controversial to some of us who, having grown up academically in English departments, have tacitly learned that there is, and is supposed to be, a considerable difference and distance between writer and reader. While literary academicians and fiction writers are often wary of each other, one point on which both camps can agree is to be suspicious of anyone who talks about the needs of readers. Because of this reluctance to consider the reader, the field was slow to respond to reader response criticism with its attention to the reader's role in creating meaning in a text. The writer who pays conscious attention to what readers want risks being labeled negatively as at best, a journalist, and at worst, a hack. Writers such as Gertrude Stein, William Faulkner, and Virginia Woolf have explicitly denounced the importance of considering readers' needs or desires. "The predominant fashion among serious writers," Wayne Booth explains in *The Rhetoric of Fiction*, "has been to consider any recognizable concern for the reader as a commercial blemish on the otherwise spotless face of art."[9]

The separateness of writer and reader has not always been so pronounced, however, nor will it necessarily remain that way. Authors' attitudes towards readers do change over time; Wayne Booth notes that Anthony Trollope, for instance, thought it was his duty to "make himself pleasant" by making his meaning available to readers (p. 90). Even among contemporary writers, the supposed ideal of the audience-free writer, unconcerned about the needs of readers, is belied by the actual processes by which writers compose. Reputable authors regularly solicit opinions about their manuscripts from friends, colleagues, agents, and editors, and they often take those opinions into account during revisions. Furthermore, once a text has been published, according to literary critics such as Stanley Fish and Louise Rosenblatt, readers as members of interpretive communities play an active role in creating its meaning. Thus, writers, readers, and texts are inextricably connected.

In the case of certain arts, such as film-making—witness the lengthy list of credits—the collaboration of a number of people is obvious. Furthermore, the presence of the audience as a collective, responsive group is also apparent; people tend to see movies in groups, while they read books or look at paintings individually. Still, as Janet Wolff explains in *The Social Production of Art*, "the notion of art as collective applies also to those arts which appear most 'private' and individual."[10] Wolff uses the case of writers to exemplify this paradox: "Even writers need materials, need to be literate, benefit from acquaintance with some literary tradition and conventions . . . and need access to publishers and printers, as well as being [sic] affected by both the book market and (possibly) literary critics. The simple idea of an artistic idea being penned (in whatever form) by an inspired individual, and then made available for recognition and consumption by the waiting audience/reader begins to recede into the realm of myth."[11]

From this perspective, then, the notion that a writer or artist creates in isolation from society and culture is seen as a distortion of how art and literature are actually made. Says Margaret Atwood, in regard to fiction writing: "Writer and audience are Siamese twins. Kill one and you run the risk of killing the other. Try to separate them, and you may simply have two dead half-people."[12] Barbara Tuchman says in reference to her writing about history: "If I seem to stress the reader's interest rather more than the pure urge of the writer, it is because, for me, the reader is the essential other half of the writer. Between them is an indissoluble connection. If it takes two to make love or war or tennis, it likewise takes two to complete the function of the written word. I never feel my writing is born or has an independent existence until it is read."[13] These observations about the importance of the reader seem equally applicable to what is commonly thought to be more "functional" writing, such as technical writing or business communication. Whether one's goal is nonfiction or a novel, then, a view of invention as an act connects a writer with readers who bring the process to completion.

Inventing over Time

In addition to considering the necessary bridge between inventor and audience, a view of invention as an act emphasizes that inventing, whether in a rhetorical or a generic sense, often involves a series of social transactions and texts that may extend over time. By contrast, modern composition studies have concentrated on the individual writer's composition of a single text as a product that serves as the focal point for both teaching and research. Over the past two decades, however, composition teaching and research have begun to encompass the creation and revison of texts over time. More recently, longitudinal and naturalistic studies have also begun to go beyond texts to examine the interactions of writers with others during composing processes that are tracked over an extended period of time.[14]

This significant trend away from isolating a single episode of composing and instead conceiving of writing and inventing as extending over time through a series of transactions and texts may be seen as having theoretical support in the work of a number of contemporary philosophers, historians, and literary critics. Michel Foucault, for instance, in his "Discourse on Language," describes the beginning of a discourse as a re-emergence into an ongoing, never-ending process: "At the moment of speaking, I would like to have perceived a nameless voice, long preceding me, leaving me merely to enmesh myself in it. . . . There would have been no beginnings: instead, speech would proceed from me, while I stood in its path—a slender gap—the point of its possible disappearance."[15] Elaborating on this perspective, one may come to regard discourse not as an isolated event, but rather a constant potentiality that is occasionally evidenced in speech or writing. The beginnings and ends of rhetorical acts are thus not clearly obvious or absolute.

In fact, as the work of historian Fernand Braudel suggests, the definition of what constitutes an act or event should be carefully considered lest we create misleading demarcations by dividing experience arbitrarily into discrete units. Braudel contrasts two major views of history: history as a series of discrete events and history as a continuum of enduring forces and structures. According to Braudel, history has traditionally erred in concentrating too much on a narrative history, the history of events occurring in a short time span or episode—*l'histoire événementielle.*[16] Individual persons and episodic events do not exclusively shape history; larger, less obvious movements may shape individuals and events. Individuals are always rooted in a more complex reality, one that is slower to change, fairly constant: analogous, perhaps, to the ostinato that forms a constant and perceptible background in a musical composition, one which nevertheless counterpoints the shorter, more obvious episodes that occur over it. For Braudel, this slower-paced history—the *"longue durée"*—can include geographical and economic limits, mental frameworks, biological constants, and unconscious history. These change very slowly and are nearly motionless, Braudel acknowledges, but they nevertheless exert a constant pressure. They are like deep ocean currents beneath the quicker, sharper surface waves.[17]

Like Foucault's type of discourse that "remains spoken, indefinitely, beyond its formulation" (p. 220) and may have enduring effects, Braudel's *longue durée* calls attention to the undercurrent forces or structures that continue to affect history. Such perspectives suggest that traditional views of an event or act have been mis-leading when they have presumed that the individual unit—a speech or a written text, an individual hero, a particular battle or discovery—is clearly separable from a larger, continuing force or stream of events in which it participates. For similar reasons Jacques Derrida has criticized literary theories that attempt to explain the meaning of a text apart from other texts that precede and follow it. "What is significant," Foucault explains, "is that history does not consider an event without defining the series to which it belongs" (p. 230).

What is also significant, I would argue—especially in light of views advanced in modern theoretical physics, claiming that the very act of observing a phenomenon changes it—is that in defining the individual unit, one must consider the perspective and purpose of its definer. As John Dewey has said, "For some purposes, for some results, the tree is the individual, for others the cell, and for a third, the forest or landscape" (p. 187). Put in terms of tagmemics, one field's particle is another particle's field. In investigating the in-vention process of individuals who are necessarily social beings as well, it is misleading to focus exclusively on the "particle" of the spatially separate inventor and the spatially separate text. Invention is more comprehensively viewed if it is conceived as an ongoing pro-cess—a *longue durée*—occurring in individuals and groups, which is occasionally manifested in an event such as a speech or a written text.

To put this perspective into practice, let us imagine that we are observing a writer at her desk, at work on an article for a profes-sional journal. In drafting notes that eventually become fuller texts, she perhaps subjects her ideas to the scrutiny of an imaginary reader, modifying them by means of internal dialogue. Later she asks a colleague to respond to a draft. As they discuss ideas, new thoughts begin to form. Back the writer goes to another draft, an-other imaginary reader, and yet another actual reader. Eventually the editor of a journal reads the article, suggesting changes and ad-ditions. A year later it is published. Readers write responses to the editor; the writer composes her defense. The text is "finished"— except that the process has provoked a new idea that the writer may use in another article. Perhaps her article prompts someone else to develop ideas in a different direction. For both writer and reader, then, the closure of one series of talks and texts may end in invention.

Such a progression over time through various types of social interaction is not always so clear-cut, of course, but it does happen. The cycle of writing that extends through revision is often a "social act," as Christopher Gould and Karen Hodges note: it involves "interactions among writer, writer-as-reader, other readers, and the constraints of their society and text."[18] These interactions of revising often generate further invention as part of an ongoing social process. Yet if we had looked at our hypothetical article writer at her desk, alone, on a Sunday night, with not even the radio for company, we might have concluded on the basis of a single observation that invention is a private, asocial act.

That invention is *not* an asocial act is seen even more dramatically in a very different instance of invention: the generation of ideas that occurs through what is called a "one-text" negotiating procedure. This procedure, which was used to negotiate the Camp David Accords between Israeli prime minister Menachem Begin and Egyptian president Anwar Sadat, has been defined by negotiator Roger Fisher as "a process of successive nonbinding drafts of a discussion text to which no one is committed."[19] At Camp David, a team of American mediators interviewed both the Egyptian and Israeli delegations to determine their positions regarding the Sinai Peninsula, as well as their underlying interests. The Americans then created a draft of a text and met separately with each side. After each meeting, the negotiating text was revised in light of the criticism received. After twenty-three revisions, the American team formulated an actual proposal, phrased so that it could be answered by a yes or no: they proposed a demilitarized Sinai that would return to Egypt's rule, thus achieving security for Israel and sovereignty for Egypt. Begin and Sadat each agreed to accept this proposed text if the other would.[20]

While this process is called a "one-text" procedure, it obviously involves not one but many written drafts, numerous discussions, and successive invention sessions held over a period of time. Rhetorical abilities are clearly required here, to invent, argue, mediate, speak, and write. Yet an American diplomat or negotiator or citizen would not have learned about discussion texts or collaborative invention in a rhetoric and composition class. More likely they would have learned that invention is a private act of an individual who expresses innate ideas, and it is doubtful that such instruction would have benefited this situation. This negotiation process exemplifies an important type of collaborative invention occurring in constrained circumstances. While collaborative invention is increasingly necessary on both local and global levels, it is overlooked or even misrepresented in contemporary composition theory and practice. Viewing invention as a social act thus draws our attention to the importance of studying and teaching invention in new ways, both in and out of the composition class.

Classical Precedents for a Social Perspective on Invention

Viewing invention from a social rather than a Platonic perspective may at first seem unorthodox. To say that invention is best understood as a social act goes against the grain of our capitalistic and individualistic tendencies. Maintaining that human consciousness and creativity are affected by social structures may seem to move us into Marxist territory. It seems to weaken the power of the individual, and that appears to be downright anti-democratic. It sounds as if all ideas are created by committee. In fact, however, a social perspective on rhetorical invention does not deprive the individual of rights or responsibilities, and it is not quite as new and unusual as it may at first seem. It is compatible with certain of Plato's ideas and to a greater extent, Aristotle's, and thus has precedents in classical rhetoric. Before going on to propose a theoretical continuum for a view of invention as a social act, I would like to acknowledge its roots in classical rhetoric.

As I have suggested previously, Plato's view of the individual as seeker of knowledge is paradoxical: it may be seen as both asocial and social. Plato has two theories of the self, Richard McKeon tells us: the self as motivated by and taking part in the (futile) attempt to realize an ideal form or an ideal representation of itself; and the self as both a product and a motivator in a dialectic between the individual and the larger—social, political, cosmological—environment.[21]

The first theory, underlying Plato's myth of the soul's journey to the realm of ideal forms, is the basis for what I have described as an asocial view of the individual absorbed in the private task of recollecting truth. Plato's second theory concerning the self—the self as both product and motivator of a dialectic with a larger sphere—is compatible with the social perspective on invention that I elaborate in this study. This view includes the process of Socratic dialogue as a way of knowing by interacting with opposites and with others. The concept of a dialogical interaction with internalized or actual others does suggest that a significant social dimension can be traced back to classical rhetoric.

To a greater extent than Plato, the views of Aristotle support a rhetorical perspective that emphasizes social elements. Aristotle's *Rhetoric* presupposes a social context. Aristotle's three kinds of rhetoric (deliberative, forensic, and epideictic) are determined in reference to others as "three kinds of hearers."[22] Aristotle defines rhetoric as the art of finding the available means of persuasion, which means that it must involve others who are to be persuaded. The three kinds of proofs—ethos, logos, pathos—by which the rhetor persuades similarly presuppose the existence of others who may or may not accept certain proofs. The audience is actively involved in building the argument in that the rhetor must look to the audience to supply the premises of the enthymemes on which the argument rests. In this broad sense, then, Aristotle's view of rhetoric and of the sources one should use to invent rhetorical arguments may be called social in its orientation and purpose.

Perhaps most pertinent to a social perspective is Aristotle's concept of ethos. For Aristotle, ethos refers not to the idiosyncracies of an individual, and not to a personal and private construct such as is often meant by "personality"; rather, ethos arises from the relationship between the individual and the community. "Ethos," says Karlyn Kohrs Campbell, "does not refer to your peculiarities as an individual but to the ways in which you reflect the characteristics and qualities that are valued by your culture or group."[23] In Aristotle's view, ethos cannot exist in isolation; by definition it requires possible or actual others. Most of classical rhetoric involved spoken rather than written discourse, so the actual presence of others as audience would have been obvious. As S. Michael Halloran notes, ethos in the Aristotelian sense emphasizes the public rather than the private; in fact, the Greek meaning for "ethos" as "a habitual gathering place" calls forth an image of people coming together.[24] In written composition, the social matrix of necessary others who form community and audience is less obvious, but nevertheless present. Ethos, we might say, appears in that socially created space, in the "between," the point of intersection between speaker or writer and listener or reader.

By virtue of the ethos or moral character that a rhetor imparts, he influences his listeners. Ideally this ethos is manifested in the virtues valued by his culture, virtues that Aristotle lists for us—justice, courage, and so forth. The values Aristotle promotes in the *Rhetoric* are clearly influenced by the concept of the human being as one-among-others. "The greatest virtues," Aristotle tells us, "are necessarily those which are the most useful to others, if virtue is the faculty of conferring benefits" (*Rhetoric*, I.ix.1366b). Acts done for others are judged more favorably than those done for oneself, as are successes gained for others, and acts of kindness. "The height of virtue, " Aristotle says, "is to do good to all." Indeed, arguments are all judged according to the social context in which they are made: "As Socrates said, it is not difficult to praise Athenians among Athenians" (*Rhetoric*, I.ix.1367b).

For Aristotle, an individual's character is created and expressed by virtue of that person's existence in a community. In inventing arguments, the rhetor tries to manifest sound character; what he is will be reflected in, or possibly even created by, what he says; and what he says and what he is will be judged according to the virtues valued by a group of people. Rhetorical invention thus cannot be viewed as a totally private act of an individual. It presupposes the existence of others and is oriented to take into account their knowledge, attitudes, and values.

A view of invention as a social act, then, is compatible with prominent classical and contemporary theoretical perspectives. In summary, to think of invention as a social act is to regard it in the following ways:

- as actively creating—as well as finding or remembering—that which is the substance of discourse;
- as involving a variety of social relationships with real and imaginary others, with individuals as well as social collectives;
- as a dialectical process in which individuals interact with socioculture in a unique way to generate something;

- as an act that generally is initiated by inventors and brought to completion by an audience, often extending over time through a series of social transactions and texts.

In contrast to the accent a Platonic view places on the atomistic inventor, a social perspective stresses the dialectical relationship of the individual with society and culture. The next chapter will propose a theoretical framework that permits us to examine both Platonic and social inventional perspectives, in theory as well as practice, in the composition class and across the curriculum.

4

A Continuum of
Social Perspectives
on Invention

Overview of the Continuum

If we think of invention as a social act involving a dialectical relationship between individual and social spheres, what theoretical framework can we employ to study it? The scheme I propose is a four-part continuum of perspectives on invention: Platonic, internal dialogic, collaborative, and collective views. This continuum extends from a view of invention as an act of an atomistic individual, through intrapersonal and interpersonal perspectives, to invention as influenced by the supra-individual entity of a social collective. In its movement from the individual to the collective, the continuum is analogous to that used by James Moffett, whose categories of discourse include reflection (communication within one individual); conversation (two people speaking); correspondence (communicating between remote people or small groups who know each other somewhat); and publication (communicating over space and time to an anonymous large group).[1] Moffett's scheme, however, is concerned with the distance between writer and audience as related to the type of discourse, while the continuum I present offers instead a range of ways to explore the social elements of invention.

I classify these social elements in four main groups to arrest these dynamic processes temporarily in order to study them. Of course, there is not really such a neat separation of invention into types or phases. This is a continuum, not a set of categories. More than one of these social relationships may exist when a writer invents, and more than one of these perspectives may be operating in the work of a single composition theorist. Indeed, it is perhaps to be expected that some composition theories and pedagogies will overlap perspectives on this continuum. S. Michael Halloran has pointed out that in terms of the history of thought, we are in a transition away from a positivist view of the world, and thus it is not surprising to find that a theory might include, for instance, a mixture of Platonic and dialogical elements, even though the assumptions underlying these perspectives differ.[2] A theorist may have a foot in both camps, creating both real and apparent contradictions, while "trying out" a new approach. Given these transitions, it is also difficult in some cases to examine pedagogical practices or textbooks and deduce their underlying assumptions. A teacher who adds a few group activities to the composition classroom does not automatically have a dialectical view of invention. Reconceiving invention as a social act does not mean simply that we assemble a group of atomistic individuals— "add people and stir"—who later resume their private search for knowledge. On the other hand, a scholar whose focus of study is a single writer need not necessarily hold a Platonic view of invention; the study might regard that individual as a participant in a dialectical interchange with other people and with socioculture.

Difficult though it may be to determine underlying assumptions, some type of analysis is necessary if we are to investigate the invention process, as well as existing theories of invention, to see what emphasis is or is not placed on social elements in invention. Rather than divide the field into adversarial and mutually exclusive camps, I prefer to use a continuum that allows us to recognize degrees of emphasis and overlapping views. To illustrate the main assumptions behind each of four perspectives on invention, I will describe in each case a model used by a major social thinker whose work is representative of that perspective. To illustrate the broad applicability of this continuum to the study of invention in both its rhetorical and generic senses, I have drawn examples of the development of new ideas from diverse areas: science, mathematics, business, literature, psychology, and art.

1. **Platonic perspective.** Based on Plato's myth of the soul's journey to the realm of ideal forms, this perspective concerns invention

as a private, asocial activity engaged in by an individual who possesses innate knowledge to be recollected and expressed, or innate cognitive structures to be projected onto the world.

2. Internal dialogic perspective. Illustrated by Freud's model of the psyche with its superego that internalizes social dictates in the individual, this view maintains that invention is largely a process of internal dialogue or dialectic with another "self," often involving internalized constructs influenced by external social forces and actual people.

3. Collaborative perspective. Based on George Herbert Mead's explanation of the making of meaning (as a result of the interaction of three elements: actions or gestures; resulting interpretations of gestures; and responses of the self and others to gestures), a collaborative view maintains that people interact to invent and to create a resonating environment for inventors.

4. Collective perspective. Founded on Emile Durkheim's concept of the power of the social collective as a supra-individual entity, the collective view is based on an assumption that invention is neither a purely individual nor an interpersonal act or process; rather, it is encouraged or constrained by social collectives whose views are transmitted through such things as institutions, societal prohibitions, and cultural expectations.

Since I have previously discussed the first perspective on this continuum—a Platonic view of invention—I will say no more about it here. The rest of this chapter explains and illustrates the remaining three perspectives: internal dialogic, collaborative, and collective views of invention (see table 1). In contrast to Platonic invention, these three views acknowledge varying social elements in invention. In discussing these views, I will consider the assumptions and methods of several composition theorists and teachers to see to what extent and in what ways their work seems to be consistent with a view of invention as a social act. Some of the systems of invention frequently cited in composition literature will not receive detailed analysis here as representing one perspective or another. These broad systems—including Aristotle's *topoi*, Kenneth Burke's pentad, Jacqueline Berke's twenty questions for the writer, Richard L. Larson's questions to aid invention, and the journalist's five W's—could, it seems to me, be used for invention from a variety of perspectives, depending on the assumptions on which their use is based and the ways in which they are put into practice. For instance, I have suggested that Aristotle's views are in important ways compatible with a social perspective on invention. Yet Aristotle's *topoi* have on occasion been used as the basis for what turns out to be a Platonic view, as in D'Angelo's early work, which maintains that the *topoi* are analogous to innate conceptual categories that are the basis for invention. Furthermore, the *topoi* could be used by two or more collaborators inventing together. Thus, a broad inventional scheme need not be considered inherently Platonic or social; what matters is the way the scheme is interpreted and used.

Both extremes on this continuum—the Platonic and collective views—are to some extent oversimplifications of the invention process, much as any implied dichotomy between individual and social perspectives is ultimately a fiction. An individual cannot be totally divorced from social collectives any more than a social collective can be totally separated from individuals. Nevertheless, such divisions on this continuum are useful ways of showing differing degrees of emphasis in theories or teaching practices. The Platonic view stresses the inventor as an atomistic unit expressing truths found within; the collective, the inventor as a vehicle conveying ideas imposed from without. Opposed to these extremes on the continuum are the dialectical views, which emphasize the importance for invention of interactions with real or internalized others. Dialectical views should be particularly applicable in light of post-positivist attempts to understand human beings as active participants in the creation and use of knowledge.

While each perspective on the continuum provides us with useful insights about the nature of invention in general and rheorical invention in particular, I think it will become apparent that composition as a field has given more than a fair share of acknowledgment to the Platonic and internal dialogic views of invention; it has only recently paid some attention to collaborative views; and it has virtually ignored collective views. The slighting of these last two perspectives—the absence of a theoretical scheme of models of invention that would allow us even to recognize their existence—is something that requires correction if we hope to have a comprehensive understanding of what happens when writers invent.

Table 1

Perspectives on Rhetorical Invention

Perspective	Platonic	Internal Dialogic	Collaborative	Collective
Social Theorist	Plato	Sigmund Freud	George Herbert Mead	Emile Durkheim
	Individual is agent of invention.		Two or more people interact to invent.	Invention influenced by social collectives.
Emphasis for Invention	Invent by recollecting or finding and expressing content or cognitive structures that are innate. Asocial mode of invention; internal locus of evaluation of what is invented.	Invent through internal dialogue or dialectic with construct of internalized other. Internal locus of evaluation, but influenced by internalized social codes and values.	Invent by interacting with people who allow developing ideas to resonate and who indirectly or directly support inventors. Listeners and readers receive and thus complete the act of invention. Locus of evaluation may be one person influenced by judgments of others, or a pair or group of people who invent together.	Invention is hindered or encouraged by the force of supra-individual collectives. Locus of evaluation is a social unit beyond the individual (e.g. an organization, bureaucracy, or socio-culture).

Examples				
D'Angelo's cognitive analogues of the topoi as structures for inventing.	D'Angelo's use of dialogue to aid invention and the inventor's development.	Macrorie's "helping circle" groups.	Ohmann, Yarnoff: The need to relate invention to material, social, and political spheres.	
Tagmemic matrix with its conceptual universals.	Young, Becker, and Pike: Writing as an internal transaction between writer and world. Writer's concern for imagined audience in Rogerian argument.	Bruffee's collaborative learning groups. Peer tutoring. Murray's process-centered writing conferences. Elbow's teacherless writing groups.	Marcuse: The collective closes the universe of discourse.	
Macrorie's "authentic self."				
Rohman and Wlecke: invention as organic development of a "seed idea."	Murray: Writer's dialogue with "other self."	Synectics groups. Business and industry: products and documentation created with ideas from users.	Ludwik Fleck's "thought collective."	
Murray: "inner voice" that leads writers to meaning.			Gerald Holton's themata.	
Expressive powers latent in the right hemisphere of the brain.	Left brain/right brain relationship influencing invention.	Team science. Business proposals. Contracts and treaties. Political platforms. Frances Steloff and the Gotham Book Mart. Sylvia Beach's Shakespeare and Company. Freud's disciples.	Collective seal of approval: admission to/exclusion from professional organizations (e.g. women in science).	
Elbow's "real self" and "real voice."	Elbow's inner dialogue of "you" with "not you"; dialectic between doubt and belief that generates ideas.		Durkheim's social facts. Virginia Woolf's collective community of women writers.	
			T. S. Eliot: the collective entity of the writer's "tradition."	

Invention as Internal Dialogue

This perspective on rhetorical invention emphasizes the role of internal dialogue within the rhetor as a chief method by which he or she thinks and invents. Like Platonic invention, the internal dialogic view accents the individual person and does not presuppose that overt social transactions with others necessarily play a direct part in the invention process. However, unlike a Platonic view, which sees invention as the projection of an inner, atomistic self, the internal dialogic view holds that the individual invents by carrying on an inner conversation or dialectic with another "self" that also functions as a bridge to the rest of the social world. This internal partner often acts as a monitor and guide; it may function as a construct embodying features of one's audience. Even though the agent of invention is an individual, invention according to this view is affected and indeed made possible by an "otherness" that is dynamically present in each I.

Theoretical Foundation: Sigmund Freud

Freud's model of the individual psyche as a dynamic interplay of forces emphasizes the inner life but at the same time attempts to account for the influence of the social world on the individual. Psychoanalysis has always made much of Freud's concentration on the study of individuals and their subjective interpretations. Yet even as Freud concerned himself with the individual, he also recognized the influence of social context. Some of Freud's earlier work (e.g., "The Aetiology of Hysteria," 1896) claimed that harmful social experience, such as child abuse, was responsible for subsequent neurosis in adults. Recently Freud has come under renewed criticism for later repudiating this seduction theory in the face of opposition from his colleagues and claiming instead that such experiences are really imagined.[3] Whether or not he deserves this criticism, it is clear that his work reflects ambivalence about the relationship between the individual psyche and the social realm. Positing the existence of the superego was a chief way that Freud represented in his theory a structure that incorporates social and cultural forces in the psyche of the individual.

Freud's own invention—in the dialectical tradition shared by thinkers such as Anaximander, Heraclitus, Socrates, and Marx—is a theory of an internal dialectic going on in the unconscious, involving the interplay of the ego, the superego, and the id. According to Freud, when a child is approximately five years old, the ego (representing reason and the guidance of common sense) identifies with some portion of the external world and takes it into the ego, where it continues to function as part of one's internal world. This internalized construct of the superego, incorporating the standards of parents, social class, religion, and culture, both rewards and punishes the ego for its acts, wishes, thoughts, and intentions.[4] The superego is a bridge to the social world even as it remains a part of the inner world, influencing the internal negotiations of the ego and id.

Employing Freud's model as an analogue for one view of rhetorical invention allows us to pay special attention to the inner dynamics occurring when a writer invents. My purpose here is not to analyze the cognitive processes associated with invention; however, a model that allows for debate, dissension, and consideration of alternative views does seem appropriate when one is concerned with invention. A pattern of thinking that involves some form of opposition is characteristic of the creative process in many fields. Dialectical thinking, which alternately considers a thesis and antithesis and seeks a synthesis among disparate elements, has long been regarded as a method of intellectual discovery.

In a recent study of the creative process, Albert Rothenberg proposes another kind of oppositional thinking contributing to creativity: janusian thinking, a process in which two or more antitheses coexist and operate simultaneously.[5] In regard to scientific creativity, for instance, Rothenberg cites historian of science Gerald Holton's claim that science always has two or more coexisting sets of antithetical systems, and that "scientists of genius" must have a "special sensitivity to contraries." Often, Holton argues, an important scientific discovery involves a reconceptualizing of just what the opposites are thought to be. For instance, Einstein showed that matter and energy are not antitheses but are really synonymous or interchangeable.[6]

While thinking through contraries is a method often used to create and test new ideas, the internal dialogic model used here does not require that the inner conversation be in terms of opposites. The main feature of this model is that it conceives of ideas as generated through a dialogue—sometimes a dialectic: call it an idealogue—going on within an individual. This process is represented in an internalized social construct that both is and is not a part of the self. While this inner actor or other self may derive from social influences and actual others whom one has known, once it has been internalized it may evolve further on its own; as Freud notes, "It is a remarkable thing that the superego often displays a severity for which no model has been provided by the real parents."[7] In this internal dialogic view, the locus of evaluation, whether it be the evaluation of behavior or ideas, lies within the individual but is also influenced by the social world from which it came.

The Greeks knew of this sort of internal monitor with which a part of the self converses while on the way to a new idea. In *The Life of the Mind*, Hannah Arendt discusses Socrates' view of thought as a dialogue of the two-in-one carried on in the mind, and Plato's translation of the concept into "the soundless dialogue—*eme emauto*—between me and myself." "It is this *duality* of myself with myself," Arendt explains, "that makes thinking a true activity, in which I am both the one who asks and the one who answers. Thinking can become dialectical and critical because it goes through this questioning and answering process, through the dialogue of *dialegesthai*, which is actually a 'traveling through words.'"[8]

The close connection of the thinking individual to social context is further suggested by the image of the *daimonion*, an inner monitor and partner in thought. To the Greeks, the *daimonion* (or daimon) personifies one's true identity; it is an "other self" that is intimately involved in thinking. A person can never actually see her own daimon, which perches behind the left shoulder and can thus be seen only by others. One who lives virtuously projects to others a virtuous daimon. While the daimon, like the superego, serves as an internal guide, the daimon has a more positive connotation of helping to generate thought. It is sometimes thought to be a source of writers' ideas, as is Kipling's Daemon that lives in makers' pens: "if he be utterly present, and they swerve not from his behest, / the word that he gives shall continue, whether in earnest or jest."[9] Both daimon and superego occupy an intermediary position between the self and others; each at some stage requires others in order to exist. The superego derives its standards, at least originally, from the social world; the daimon is fully realized only when it is recognized by others. The constructs of superego and daimon supply metaphors that show how thought can be at the same time individual and social, and how it can occur through a dynamic interplay, an inner dialogue. As Wayne Booth says, "Even when thinking privately, 'I' can never escape the other selves which I have taken in to make 'myself,' and my thought will always be a dialogue."[10]

Social psychologists who use an internal dialogic model for their own purposes speak in terms familiar to rhetoricians. For early twentieth century sociologist Charles Horton Cooley, higher thought, which generally involves language, is always a kind of internalized "imaginary conversation": "The life of the mind," he says, "is essentially a life of intercourse."[11] For Cooley, an isolated self is an impossibility because the self is created through communication with others. While Cooley still emphasizes the individual's mental constructions of society (seeing "facts of society" as synonymous with "the imagination people have of one another"),[12] he paves the way, as we shall see, to the more overtly interpersonal emphasis of George Herbert Mead and eventually to the emphasis on society as an abstract collective in the work of Emile Durkheim.

The importance of internalized others is also stressed by American psychiatrist Harry Stack Sullivan, whose interpersonal theory of psychiatry maintains that the formation of the self depends in part on a dynamic process in the individual, involving internalized others. From experience with overt interpersonal relations, Sullivan says, the juvenile develops covert patterns in his self-system. These are "supervisory patterns" or "'really' imaginary people who are always with one" and who often take the form of internal critics—readers of one's own writing, listeners to one's talk—who may help or hinder a person. "It is as if there were two people," Sullivan says, "one who actually utters statements, and another who attempts to see that what is uttered is fairly well adjusted to its alleged purpose."[13] Such constructs continue to evolve throughout one's life. They may be derived from actual people one has known, from "eidetic" or imagined people, or from a blend of both. Especially pertinent to composition is Sullivan's example of the effect that one of his own supervisory patterns, that of "reader," has on his writing:

> He's a charming pill, practically entirely responsible for the fact that I almost never publish anything. He is bitterly paranoid, a very brilliant thinker, and at the same time an extraordinarily wrongheaded imbecile.

Thus when I attempt to use the written language to communicate serious thought, I am unhappily under constant harassment to so hedge the words around that the most bitterly critical person will be unable to grossly misunderstand them, and, at the same time, to make them so clear that this wrongheaded idiot will grasp what I'm driving at.[14]

Like Sullivan, W. H. Auden talks of an inner critic. Auden's "internal Censor" of his poetry provides helpful correction and is more like a "Censorate": "It should include, for instance, a sensitive only child, a practical housewife, a logician, a monk, an irreverent buffoon and even, perhaps, hated by all the others and returning their dislike, a brutal, foul-mouthed drill sergeant who considers all poetry rub bish."[15] For writers whose invention is hindered by too severe a critic, teachers often recommend brainstorming as a means of suspending temporarily this critical dialogue so that new ideas are given a chance to reveal their merits.

Internal Dialogue and Composition Theory

A number of researchers and theorists base their work on the assumption that some form of internal conversation goes on within the writer. According to Carl Bereiter and Marlene Scardamalia, children learn to write by gradually internalizing the interactive process and patterns they have previously learned from conversation with others. The development of writing ability is made possible by a transformation from a socially interactive to an autonomous process, a movement "from conversation to composition."[16] L. S. Vygotsky's theory that thought is a form of inner speech internalized from social speech also stresses a development of inner cognitive processes from social patterns and practices.[17] Linda Flower uses Vygotsky's work (as well as Piaget's) as a basis for her discussion of "writer-based prose," defined as "a verbal expression written by a writer to himself and for himself."[18] The research technique of protocol analysis—analyzing recordings of a writer thinking aloud during composing—advocated by Flower and John R. Hayes presumes and helps to document the existence of writers' internal dialogues.

The system of tagmemic invention as presented by Richard Young, Alton Becker, and Kenneth Pike in *Rhetoric: Discovery and Change* also has certain characteristics that are compatible with an internal dialogic perspective. As the following quotation suggests, tagmemic invention presumes that a transaction between problem-solving writer and world occurs within the writer's mind: "Constantly changing, bafflingly complex, the external world is not a neat, well-ordered place replete with meaning, but an enigma requiring interpretation. This interpretation is the result of a transaction between events in the external world and the mind of the individual—between the world 'out there' and the individual's previous experience, knowledge, values, attitudes, and desires.[19] Tagmemic invention, according to Richard Young, fuses concerns for the writer's discovery and the audience's reaction. "Pre-writing [Rohman and Wlecke] focuses on the discovery of ordering principles and on psychological changes in the writer," Young points out; "classical invention focuses on finding arguments which are likely to produce psychological changes in the audience. Tagmemic invention focuses on both."[20]

Tagmemic invention is also dialogic in its advocacy of Rogerian argument, a process by which a writer identifies with an opponent's point of view in order to reduce the opponent's sense of being threatened and to enable the inventor to understand the problem from another point of view. In effect, the process can help a writer to think with an imagined other about the problem at hand. The Rogerian method, as Charles Yarnoff points out, presents "writing as provisional self-communication rather than self-expression or argumentation."[21] Rogerian argument is thus an invention procedure that takes into account the ideas and values of others as the writer imagines them to be.

While the general orientation of tagmemic invention is in accord with the internal dialogic perspective, it also retains certain characteristics that are compatible with a Platonic view of invention. One of Kenneth Pike's tagmemic principles holds that the particle-wave-field matrix is based on constructs in human rationality that form the universal basis for human experience.[22] Using tagmemics, the inventor apparently projects those universal constructs from within onto a phenomenon or problem in the world. As with other theories based on a Platonic view, tagmemic invention thus presupposes an innate structure, with invention moving from the inside out.

The tagmemic system may furthermore be seen as Platonic in its reliance on a psychological model of the process of inquiry that draws heavily on Graham Wallas's preparation-incubation-illumination-verification sequence (described in Young et al., *Rhetoric: Discovery and Change*, pp. 73–77). The use of this model conveys the impression that a writer carries out these stages of investigation largely as an atomistic unit. Tagmemic invention shows little concern with, for instance, a writer's collaboration with others or interactions with a social collective that might encourage the solution of certain problems and discourage the solution of others. Thus, on the continuum I have described, tagmemic invention seems to be most appropriately regarded as overlapping the Platonic and internal dialogic perspectives, with emphasis on the latter. It does not involve actual others as collaborative invention would, but neither does it conceive of the individual as primarily concerned with self-expression, as do a number of pedagogical works based on a Platonic perspective.

Both Platonic and internal dialogic views are likewise the basis for Donald M. Murray's descriptions of the inventing writer. A Platonic view seems to underlie his descriptions of writers' attempts "to make meanings"—an expression that for Murray seems closely related to invention. Meaning resides somewhere in the writer, and the writer's goal is to "discover" it there, or, more accurately, to get out of the way and allow the writing to let the meaning emerge. Writing about revision, Murray observes that each change in wording, each line left out, "is an attempt to understand, to remember what I did not know I remembered."[23] The writer's task is thus to recollect what lies within, much as Plato's soul tries to remember the ideal forms it once beheld.

This sense of individual apprehension of truth intermingles with Murray's view of the writer as engaged in internal dialogue and dialectic. Four forces contend when the writer writes, Murray says: writing, collecting information and ideas, reading, and connecting what we have collected with what we know. Interacting with and counterbalancing each other, these forces constitute a dialectic that leads to invention: "These forces are in action against each other," he claims," and that action produces meaning."[24] The agents of this conflict are personified as two beings in the mind: the "writing self" and the "other self." The writing self writes for the other self that is its first reader and its monitor, providing distance from the product, commiserating, criticizing, and tracking the process.[25] When a student writer is unaware of the existence of an other self, part of the teacher's role is to help the other self manifest itself and develop. The teacher must assume that the student *has* an other self, and must address it, Murray says; the teacher in fact "models an ideal other self" and teaches it to improve its monitoring of the writing process.[26] This construct of the other self bears some resemblance to the super-ego in its role as monitor and its ability to incorporate social guidance within the individual.

Views of invention by composition theorists Frank D'Angelo and Peter Elbow similarly overlap both Platonic and internal dialogic perspectives. D'Angelo's more recent writings suggest less emphasis on the projection of innate cognitive structures in favor of a developmental view in which a writer interacts with imagined and actual others. He suggests, for instance, that students write dialogues in which they create an interchange between imagined parties. This procedure is meant to assist development by helping students move from descriptive to persuasive discourse.[27] D'Angelo also suggests that teachers interact with students to present structural paradigms based on the *topoi* to aid their invention and contribute to development of mental abilities: "The idea . . . is not merely to present students with a store of patterns, but also to get them to internalize the linguistic and conceptual principles upon which these patterns are based."[28] Here the paradigms or cognitive maps that are the basis for invention are viewed not as innate but as acquired by interaction with others and internalized in the manner described in this continuum as the internal dialogic view. The individual is still the primary agent of invention, but the inventing individual is not isolated from others.

For Peter Elbow, the writer's ideal is to express one's "real self" in a "real voice": "Look for real voice and realize it is there in everyone waiting to be used."[29] This Platonic-sounding goal of freeing oneself is often accomplished by means of internal dialogue, portrayed by Elbow as alternately doubting and believing ideas to test and develop them. This is primarily internal: "the essential transaction seems to be with oneself, a speaking to one's best self" (*Writing with Power*, p. 179). Elbow often refers to a writer's debate with an internalized audience, characterized variously as a "safe audience" that helps one think of ideas; as a "safe nonaudience" that allows suspension of an audience's "field of force" so that a writer may generate ideas without being inhibited by a sense of others; or as a "dangerous audience" that doesn't care about the writer's ideas or wants to block or change them (*Writing with Power*, p. 188). Thus, for Elbow, the writer's internal dialogue or dialectic with a part of the self or an imagined audience may be either helpful or harmful. For composition theorists who stress the concept of internal dialogue, part of what writers must learn is how to use this dialogic process to aid invention.

Invention as Collaboration

Theoretical Foundation: George Herbert Mead

With a collaborative view of rhetorical invention, we begin to be concerned with overt social relationships. People become partners in the process of creating ideas. Theoretical underpinnings for a collaborative view of invention are found in social psychologist George Herbert Mead's theory of the way meaning is made. According to Mead, meaning is not privately constructed in an individual's consciousness but is instead generated by the interaction of these three moves: (1) a gesture (in our case, a symbolic verbal gesture by an individual); (2) an attribution or interpretation of what the goal or outcome of the gesture is; and (3) a response or adjustive reaction by another individual. These three elements—gesture, resultant, response—are all essential to the creation of meaning. One person acts, and in the act of making the gesture, calls out for a response in the other. Something new is created here, Mead claims: "The response of one organism to the gesture of another . . . is the meaning of that gesture, and is also responsible for the appearance or coming into being of the new object—or new content of an old object."[30] New meanings are thus brought into existence by means of a social interaction involving a symbolic gesture and a response.

While Mead's theory is intended to explain the emergence of meaning, it also helps to show a perspective of invention that takes the invention process out of the mind of the individual and into the interaction of real people, where it may be defined as an act, a response of another individual to an initiator's gesture. Both the initiator and the respondent are collaborators in invention. In contract negotiations or business proposal writing, for example, two or more rhetors collaborate to invent, and in fact, to negotiate, a text. One person may suggest an idea; the other responds; the response becomes a gesture to the first speaker, who then generates another idea; the other responds again, and so on. One individual may initiate an idea, but without a response, the process cannot continue. Even an apparent lack of response (a long silence, a glance at the floor) is a response that figures in the action. You can't invent a contract by yourself. Eventually, each party must agree, or invention stops.

In other situations more common to writing classes we see a less perfect form of this collaborative model, but one which nevertheless involves two or more people in written or spoken dialogues that may influence invention. Examples include a peer review group, a teacher/student discussion of a student's written text, and a writer/editor critique session. In these situations, one party can override the other; e.g., a writer may decide not to include an idea suggested by a peer reader, or an editor may require a writer to make a change in content to conform to the policies of a particular publication. Whether a writer interacts with those whose roles are advisory, or collaborates with others who are equally responsible for the outcome, there is in either case an emphasis on transactions between people and on adjustive responses (as Mead would call them) on the part of both writers and readers. Something new comes about because of the ways people act with each other; inventions do not occur solely in the mind of an independent actor.

In other social thinkers, such as Martin Buber and Ludwig Wittgenstein, we find a similar emphasis on moving what have traditionally been regarded as private psychological entities out into the realm of social transactions. Early in this study I quoted Martin Buber's description of Socrates as one who even in solitude possesses an "I of infinite conversation," an I that conceives of itself as one-among-others and can internalize that transaction. That quotation may misleadingly suggest that Buber stresses internalized monologues more than he does; in fact, he emphasizes the need for interaction of real people in the world rather than imaginary encounters in the mind. Buber stresses action over essence, even suggesting that essence may be possible only through action. A self is defined dynamically as it exists in a relationship between an I and a Thou: "Man becomes an I through a You."[31] The self is not an entity, but a process. The same is true for all creation, Buber says, which reveals itself in an encounter: "it [creation] does not pour itself into senses that are waiting, but deigns to meet those that are reaching out" (p. 77). Ideas, for Buber, are not in some abstract realm, nor are they innate: "ideas are just as little enthroned above our heads as they reside within them; they walk among us and step up to us" (p. 65). Buber accents dialectical interaction: I with Thou, creation with people, ideas with thinkers—all is created dynamically, in the "between."

Buber's philosophy, Glen Matott claims, is a helpful source for teachers of composition. Matott suggests that the increasing concern in composition for the individual writer and his composing process (as opposed to his written product) has had a consequence of emphasizing self-expressiveness as a primary goal of writing. There is a likeness, Matott observes, between the contemporary stress on the isolated individual (what I have been calling a Platonic view) and Sartre's existentialism.[32] A more appropriate model for the composition teacher would be Buber, who, like Mead, accents the individual as existing, even as coming into being, through dialogue with other persons in the world.

As Mead and Buber stress the transaction of the individual with others in creating meaning and self, so does Wittgenstein in his later work stress the truly social nature of what sometimes appears to be private and individual. What we might think of as individual or psychological qualities or traits—attitudes, emotions, intentions, private language—do not receive their meanings, Wittgenstein says, from an individual whose self or mind supposedly contains or possesses them. Rather, these things derive meaning from the ways they function in situations and from the ways others respond to their use in the community. "*Essence*," Wittgenstein says, "is expressed by grammar."[33]

The theories of Mead, Buber, and Wittgenstein do of course differ in a number of ways, yet the emphasis each places on the significance of social interactions and social use in determining what something is, or what it means, or what its value may be, helps us understand why invention is appropriately considered as a social act. That is, if we extend their views to rhetorical invention, we find ourselves thinking of it not as the isolated activity of an individual who carries around ideas in a self as she carries money in a wallet and knows before she spends it exactly what it will buy. Rather, we come to think of invention as an act initiated by a person but not fully brought to fruition until it is evidenced in situations where others receive and acknowledge and eventually evaluate it. Certain acts of invention—or certain phases of inventive acts—are best understood if we think of them as being made possible by other people.

Resonance

When individuals collaborate to invent, new ideas arise in part because of a quality that I will call "resonance," a term used by Harold Lasswell. Lasswell notes that successful innovators often maintain "resonant relationships" with certain people in their social sphere. Those who are less successful innovators perhaps lack such "resonators" and may thus be more likely to succumb to the "dampening influence" of their environment.[34] A resonator, for Lasswell, may be someone who acts as a friendly audience or someone who lends financial or emotional support. Resonators might be groups of students or colleagues, accepting "apostles" who allow a person to investigate ideas in a safe place without the harsh evaluation that outsiders might make: "The withdrawal into an esoteric circle," Lasswell explains, "makes it possible to consolidate the new departure and to improve the chances of survival" (p. 217).

Resonance comes about when an individual act—a "vibration"— is intensified and prolonged by sympathetic vibrations. It may occur when someone acts as a facilitator to assist or extend what is regarded as primarily another's invention, or when people are mutual collaborators at work on a task. Resonance also occurs indirectly when people provide a supportive social and intellectual environment that nurtures thought and enables ideas to be received, thus completing the inventive act. People who act as resonators help an inventor to locate himself or herself in a tradition and a community and to live in a way that is conducive to further invention. Whether the resonating relationship is a direct collaboration or a more indirect form of support for inventors and their works, it requires the participation of real people, as opposed to the internalized others of the internal dialogic view, or the anonymous, abstract force represented in the collective perpective.

Related to this notion of resonance is a phenomenon called "clustering," which has received attention in the literature about creativity. Silvano Arieti has observed that creative genius does not appear regularly throughout history, even though one might expect there to be a constant supply of genius in individuals throughout time. Rather, Arieti tells us, "creative people who reach the rank of genius appear in particularly large numbers in certain periods of history in given geographical areas."[35] This "clustering" of creative thinkers has led some to conclude that creativity is not merely a chance manifestation of biological or psychological factors, but is subject to environmental influence. As examples, Arieti cites the proliferation of philosophy, poetry, and drama in the classic Greek period; the creativity manifested in the Italian Renaissance; the creation of a new concept of man by many people simultaneously, culminating in the American Revolution; the many contributions (especially in medicine and physics) of Jewish geniuses since the mid-nineteenth century; the contributions to psychology made during the same general period by Freud, Adler and Jung; the creativity of nineteenth century Italian opera composers (Bellini, Donizetti, Verdi, Puccini); and the post–World War II flourishing of Italian cinema (Fellini, Visconti, and Antonioni) (Arieti, pp. 294, 300, 301).

One explanation for such clustering of creativity, Arieti notes, comes from the Roman historian, Valleius Paterculus. Citing the triads of Aeschylus-Sophocles-Euripedes, and Socrates-Plato-Aristotle, Valleius suggested that people with similar talents might achieve success in similar pursuits at a given time because genius is fostered by emulation. People admire the work of another person and strive to emulate it (or to build on and criticize it, as Adler and Jung did with Freud), until the work reaches a state where further advances seem unlikely, at which point people turn to different pursuits (Arieti, p. 294). At any rate, the presence of other people engaged in similar creative work may be an impetus for one's own invention.

More recently, Charles Edward Gray (1958, 1961, 1966), building on the work of Kroeber (1944), has suggested an epicyclical theory to explain clusters of creativity. Gray maintains that history is a series of three concurrent cycles: economic, social, and political. Each cycle in turn has four stages (formative, developed, florescent, and degenerated), and rotates through these stages at different speeds. Clusters of creativity will occur when the developed and florescent stages of all three cycles coincide (Gray, in Arieti, p. 297). While I cannot here debate the validity of this and other explanations of creativity throughout history, I mention the emulation and epicyclical explanations to show that there are such hypotheses suggesting that one should not regard creativity as an innate ability but as a process occasioned or enabled by interaction with a social sphere that allows one's thoughts to resonate.

Examples of Collaborative Views

I have not attempted to work out a complete classification of the types of relationships that may exist between people who invent together or influence others' inventions. That would be a book in itself, and it would not be as appropriate for our purposes as an overview with examples to show that invention does have explicitly social elements. As research in this area progresses, we will discover various ways of analyzing and classifying collaborative types. For instance, one might focus, as Lisa Ede and Andrea Lunsford have suggested, on the different styles in which writers divide and coordinate their work: by creating and revising a text jointly; or by dividing tasks into parts for which each writer is basically responsible; or by asking members of a group to contribute sections of a document which the group together assembles and revises.[36] Another method of analysis might be to identify the key decision-makers in the social relationships. Does one individual in the relationship have the authority to adopt, adapt, or veto the ideas or information contributed by others with whom that individual interacts? Or is the power of inventing and accepting or rejecting distributed fairly equally among collaborating inventors? Such a focus could help us understand how invention may be at some times a joint social enterprise, and at others, an interaction in which people's efforts are aimed at enabling one primary agent to invent.

Leaving to future scholarship the task of conceptualizing such a system for collaborative acts, I will instead give examples of collaborations to make the point that this type of invention does indeed occur in a variety of fields and circumstances. While we are concerned at this point with collaborators with whom one might actually interact, it is essential to note that individuals are constantly collaborating in some sense with dead or absent thinkers who have paved the way for present creativity. In the case of writers, Nicholas Delbanco stresses "just how present these past masters are": "In the context of the library, collegueship extends to those one has not met—to the writers one admires. . . . The truth is that most of one's masters are dead or distant anyway: Homer and Dante and Dickens are unavailable for drinks."[37] Dead or distant, they are colleagues nonetheless in an ongoing social act.

What of invention that happens with those who *are*, so to speak, available for drinks? I will look briefly at examples of three kinds of collaborations: interactions that primarily help one person to invent; co- and group-inventions of people who are mutually involved in an enterprise; and informal relationships among people who support each other's work and make it possible for inventions to be received and thus brought to completion.

Inventing by Interaction

What I term an "interactive" type of collaboration occurs often in composition. A writer interacts with others (teachers, peers, colleagues, editors) in the course of writing and revising. Generally in this type of relationship, one person (writer, teacher, boss) has the right to make final decisions about which ideas are to be kept or changed or omitted. The principal role of others is to help the individual to generate and evaluate ideas and information.

Over the past ten years, the nature of this interaction in teaching writing has received increasing attention. For example, the workshop discussion methods presented in Peter Elbow's *Writing without Teachers* are, as the book's title suggests, an attempt to help the group find its own ways of enabling the writer to express an inner voice more fully and honestly.[38] This, too, is a main purpose in Donald Murray's teacher/student conferences, Kenneth Bruffee's collaborative learning/peer tutoring sessions, and Ken Macrorie's "helping circle" of friends or peers who react to a writer's work. In each case, the teacher and group act much as Carl Rogers' therapist functions in client-centered therapy; that is, the reader as responder helps the writer become more fully what he potentially is.

Underlying this model are the assumptions that there is something valuable and original and unspoiled in the writer, and that the reader can help to cut through stereotyped or irrelevant language and ideas so that the real writer can be heard. It is the individual writer's task to discover what is true; the purpose of the readers who interact with the writer is, as James Berlin explains, "to get rid of what is untrue to the private vision of the writer, what is, in a word, inauthentic."[39] The writer is the principal discoverer, with others serving as catalysts who make discovery possible. "The community of writers," Murray says, "instinctively understands that each piece of writing is trying to work its way towards a meaning. The community wants to help the piece of writing find its own meaning" ("Writing as Process," p. 15). "When people . . . find themselves in a group where their words are heard and understood better than they usually are," Peter Elbow observes, "they discover messages they want to send which they had forgotten were on their minds . . . which they had previously learned to ignore because it seemed impossible to get them heard" (*Writing without Teachers*, p. 123).

As an enabling agent in this process, the teacher is often advised to interact with the writer but not to usurp the writer's task of evaluation. The teacher or other reader furnishes the writer with additional information on which to base decisions. Adapting Buber's metaphor, one might say it is as if the writer's self requires a "Thou" to become an "I"; but the Thou, in this case the teacher, does not equally become an I in the process of enabling the writer. In this type of workshop or conference, the writer remains supreme, and the teacher is cautioned about interfering: "A teacher has to restrain himself or herself from providing content," Donald Murray says, "taking care not to inhibit the students from finding their own subjects, their own forms, and their own languages" ("Writing as Process," p. 3). The views of Elbow and Murray are similar in that each acknowledges the roles that other people play in assisting the writer but at the same time places emphasis on the individual inventor. Here one party exists primarily to serve the other, and while they may take turns in doing so, they are not equal partners at work on a joint project.

While this pattern of interaction—of people contributing ideas to assist someone identified as the primary agent of invention—is common in recent composition pedagogy, it is by no means restricted to that arena. Letters and biographies of a number of literary figures provide evidence that they, too, collaborate to invent, notwithstanding popular myths about the isolated writer. Caroline Gordon, for example, who after writing for a decade had been unable to complete a novel, was motivated by the encouragement of Ford Madox Ford (himself a collaborator on novels with Joseph Conrad) and by the criticism of her husband, fellow writer Allen Tate. In a letter to a friend, Gordon describes Ford's imaginative invention strategy: "Ford took me by the scruff of the neck . . . set me down in his apartment every morning at eleven o'clock and forced me to dictate at least five thousand words of my novel to him. If I complained that it was hard to work . . . he observed 'You have no passion for your art. It is unfortunate' in such a sinister way that I would reel forth sentences in a sort of panic."[40] On another occasion, while completing the same novel, *Penhally*, Gordon writes about her reaction when Allen Tate told her that the climax "would not do": "Finally I told Allen he had to write it then if it didn't suit him. He wrote a few pages and I got interested trying to fix up what he had written—it seemed to me so impossible—that I worked out of the fit."[41]

Examples of interactions that aid a writer's invention in literature and in the composition class, instructive though they may be, are not sufficiently comprehensive to further a general understanding of invention. Most of our students will do their inventing elsewhere, and it is to those contexts that we should look for further evidence of social interaction during invention. Consider, for example, invention in business and industry. The production of many technical and professional documents requires the interaction of people who specialize in different areas or lend different perspectives. A writer or, more likely, a supervisor, is ultimately responsible for deciding what to say, but the process of creating the discourse (a computer manual, for instance) would often be impossible without collaborative invention.

These collaborations are not necessarily circumscribed by company walls. According to Thomas J. Peters and Robert Waterman, who have investigated creative businesses, many new ideas come not from the isolated researcher working independently in a company's R & D lab, but from a collaboration of the company with its users. The producer has the final say and can override the ideas of users, but since the users are often the ones most familiar with how a product works in a given context, they are a rich source for new ideas. Peters and Waterman cite the research of Eric von Hippel of MIT, who investigated the source of innovation in the development of scientific instruments. Hippel found that of 11 first-of-a-type major innovations, 100 percent were invented by users rather than by the producing company's research division; of 66 major improvements to instruments, 85 percent were thought of by users; and of 83 minor improvements, two-thirds were invented by users.[42]

Peters and Waterman thus conclude that innovative companies are aware of the importance of interacting with customers whose unique perspective may lead to new ideas.

Another type of interaction used to promote creative thinking in business and industry is the group problem-solving method called synectics. Developed by W. J. J. Gordon and expanded by George M. Prince and others, synectics is a systematic procedure intended to enhance creativity in small groups. An assumption behind synectics is that some types of creative problem-solving will occur more readily in small groups operating in a certain way than in individuals working alone. Whether we work together or alone, most of us censor original ideas before they are even given a chance, George Prince explains. In a synectics group, where criticism is suspended for a time and individuals are urged to speculate without fear of having to defend themselves and their fledgling ideas, creative thinking will more likely be supported. Group members will understand the same problem differently and will concentrate on different parts of the same problem. Together they take a more comprehensive approach than they could separately. In a group in which a leader works to be sure that individuals are free from threat of attack, participants can direct their energy to inventing new ideas and building on each other's ideas rather than preserving their self-images. They need not worry about operating in what Prince describes as our traditional, unhelpful mode of action: "Compete, watch out for number one, and do it politely if possible."[43]

As described by Prince, synectics involves interaction among participants but often leaves the final evaluation and application of what is invented to a person who is regarded as an expert. This method may, however, be adapted for situations in which group members are all considered experts, or in which all are equally responsible for inventing a solution. While synectics is not specifically related to writing, it is applicable to problems that involve or result in written discourse—a grant proposal, a change in product documentation, a report. Thus, it may lead to a type of collaborative writing as well as collaborative problem-solving.

Joint Invention

Up to this point, the examples I have given of collaborations—the contributions of readers and colleagues to a writer's invention, involvement of users in industrial innovation, and interactions of synectics group members to solve an individual's problem—all illustrate ways in which one party aids what is primarily another's invention. There is another significant kind of relationship in which two or more people (or parties) invent together as true collaborators.

Writing in 1958, Henry A. Murray contended that the true individuality (as opposed to mere self-absorption) and originality that was appearing in contemporary America was often to be found, no doubt unexpectedly, in small groups. "For example," Murray says, "not only have scientists learned that cooperation is required for the solution of most problems, but they have come upon a way of thinking fruitfully in company. There is still a great deal of individual, solitary contemplation; yet it might be said that within the last twenty years the group has become the carrier of life, the unit of variation, the spearhead of evolution. A group can have individuality."[44]

Collaborative or "team" science exemplifies the type of relationship in which people are indeed expected to "think fruitfully in company." Alvin M. Weinberg, a physicist who directed the Oak Ridge National Laboratory, has argued that twentieth century science, at least as evidenced in laboratories outside academia or in certain interdisciplinary institutes within universities, has had to overcome past prejudices against team science. Investigators working in applied science, Weinberg notes, often must work in interdisciplinary teams. Whereas a scientist working in a university laboratory might decide to attempt research only in areas of his or her own expertise and work on it individually, scientists and engineers concerned with solving problems to meet the immediate demands of the everyday world cannot set such parameters. Furthermore, the knowledge and skills to solve such problems often necessitate an interdisciplinary team approach. No one person knew enough to harness atomic energy and invent the first nuclear bomb; it required the knowledge and synergy of a group of scientists working together at Los Alamos. In fields such as physics, people must work together to construct and operate complex machines. An individual who wishes to invent along certain lines must then go where there is equipment and a team. Once a team has built a complex machine, Weinberg observes, the machine itself generates ideas and directions for team research; indeed, the team plus the machine become a "powerful scientific device": "More difficult experiments can be tried with a large team equipped with a unique facility than with a smaller outfit not so equipped. Thus, insofar as breakthroughs flow from difficult experiments, one might expect teams working with powerful and unique apparatus to continue to contribute their share of important discoveries."[45]

Current research on nuclear fusion exemplifies the collaborative effort that Weinberg describes. Kenneth A. Connor, a professor of engineering at Rensselaer Polytechnic Institute who studies plasmas for fusion research, observes that such research virtually requires collaboration. According to Connor, large-scale fusion research must draw on knowledge from researchers in various fields and requires a number of people to operate sophisticated equipment in complex experiments. Furthermore, the substantial funding of millions of dollars needed for experiments with the larger new devices is awarded not to individuals but to research groups. With this type of collaborative investigation comes multiple authorship of proposals, research reports, articles, and documentation. Connor typically writes theoretical papers alone or with one other person: "This is usual for theoretical work," he says, "since most ideas need to be worked out with one other person." Most of his experimental papers have five or six authors, and sometimes more: "Many papers documenting the first good results obtained from a new experiment can have as many as twenty-five authors."[46] In certain areas of inquiry, then, collaborative invention and writing are prevalent, a fact which should inform our teaching of composition to students in science, engineering, and medicine.

Collaborative invention is not, however, restricted to certain areas of science and technology. As instances of collaborative intellectual innovation, Harold Lasswell mentions the relationship of Sigmund Freud with Professor Fliess; of Marx and Engels; of Marie and Pierre Curie; of Watson and Crick (pp. 216–17). Silvano Arieti offers another example: "Many historians agree," he says, "that if a small group of people consisting of Benjamin Franklin, George Washington, John Adams, Thomas Jefferson, John Jay, Alexander Hamilton, and James Madison had not lived and emerged at the same time, the American Revolution and the writing of the American constitution could not have taken place" (p. 323). In the writing of modern fiction and poetry, collaboration has been less frequent than in other types of writing, although as novelist John Gardner's comments about quasi collaboration mentioned earlier suggest, it may occur more often than is apparent. "I remember my astonishment as a young man," the poet and essayist Donald Hall has said, "to discover that Dylan Thomas and Vernon Watkins had rewritten each other's verse so much that there were lines by Watkins in Thomas's *Collected Poems*, and the other way around as well. I thought just us kids did it; I didn't know grown-ups did it. Well, grown-ups *do* it."[47]

In these and other instances in which invention is to be embodied in texts, collaboration can also stimulate creative thinking. Lisa Ede and Andrea Lunsford point out some of the advantages they have found in their collaborative writing of articles in rhetoric and composition. Collaborating, they say, allows them the benefits of dialectic as they question and debate with each other. It provides the stimulation of working with someone whose interests are similar and the synergy that can allow two people to create a stronger argument together than either might do alone. Coauthoring gives professors a chance to act on the ideals of collaboration and collegiality that, Ede and Lunsford note, are "much discussed but little practiced in academic life."[48] Arieti identifies the "interaction of significant persons" as one of the conditions that is necessary in a culture conducive to creativity (p. 323). People may, of course, be influenced by the products resulting from others' innovative work, but Arieti stresses the importance of interactions that are more specifically social. Two or more people, working in concert, located in the same time and place, may influence each other, increasing the chances that innovation will occur.

Sometimes we invent collaboratively because we want to—because others may provide ideas, knowledge, skills, points of view, stimulation, criticism, and motivation. Other times we invent together because we must. The teacher's union and the school board need to develop and agree upon a contract; the Democratic party caucus must create a platform for a presidential campaign; a landlord and prospective tenant must work out a lease; Egypt and Israel need to make a treaty that resolves the dispute over the Sinai. In these situations, individuals (either the negotiators or the parties directly involved) could go off into separate rooms and invent alone—but not for long. To be part of the substance of this discourse (contract, platform, lease, treaty), the ideas must be agreed upon by all parties. So, in effect, the invention must be collaborative. Further-more, not only what is invented, but by whom, and in what way, has a great deal to do with whether or not the invention is even ac-knowledged, let alone accepted.

In this arena, invention is political. Involving others in inventing is not only a way of producing more and perhaps better ideas; it is also a way of insuring that people are involved in the process of in-venting so that they have a stake in the outcome. Philip Spayd, a labor relations specialist who negotiates on behalf of the govern-ment for the Customs branch of the U.S. Treasury, notes that in cer-tain instances, it is important to pay attention to the way credit is given for ideas if one hopes to have the ideas accepted. "If I get an idea from a union person about what the union wants, " Spayd ex-plains, "and I go to 'plant' it with a government administrator, I won't say where it came from. If I say a union person thought of it, the government might not accept it." In other circumstances, it may not be productive for an objective third party to come up with an idea. "If an outside arbitrator listens to both sides and then comes up with an entirely new idea and puts that in his decision," Spayd says, "it may be unpopular with both sides since they don't have any owner-ship of it; they didn't help to make it happen." If, on the other hand, a new idea arises in a group meeting, Spayd says, "It may be better for all concerned. We have collective ownership of the new idea— *we* thought of it, and we all have an interest in seeing it work."[49] Sometimes, then, it is wise from a political point of view to create a situation in which invention is clearly a collaborative act.

Social Contexts for Invention

Yet another way of looking at collaboration is to examine the ways people associate in a community to help or hinder each other's in-ventions. To enhance the possibility that invention will occur, people must be able to work, to think, to be part of a past tradition and a continuing community, and to have their works received by others so that the inventive act is completed. Too often an "in-vention" (unacknowledged, and hence, incomplete) dies or disap-pears because clear social links are not provided. In order to de-velop new ideas, Lewis Coser has suggested, intellectuals need two things: contact with an audience whom they can address and by whom they can be acknowledged; and regular contact with others with whom they can debate ideas and evolve common standards. "The salon, the coffee house, the Royal Society—whatever their differences as institutions," Coser notes, "made face-to-face contact possible between intellectuals and their peers and audiences."[50] These largely informal associations of individuals, whether in literary Bohemia or political sects or the pages of experimental magazines, have allowed the avant-garde and the rebellious to support each other in developing new ideas even as they kept a necessary distance from those conventional thinkers whose ideas they opposed.[51]

Of the many fields that offer examples of how social links, weak or strong, between creative thinkers may influence invention, let us consider the very different arenas of genetics and literature. In genetics, only recently have researcher Barbara McClintock's discoveries regarding the rearrangement of genes during development been acknowledged by the scientific community. McClintock's biographer, Evelyn Fox Keller, approaches her subject as necessarily involving the connections between individual and community. McClintock's story, Keller says, is "above all . . . the story of one woman's conception of science that gradually—although not inevitably—isolated her from the evolving discourse of mainstream research."[52] There are several explanations for the fact that McClintock's work, which eventually won her a Nobel Prize, was ignored in the 1950s and 1960s. McClintock did her experiments with corn, which is itself unusual in contemporary genetics, and which led some to conclude that her findings about genetic transposition were peculiar to corn and not generalizable to other organisms. Furthermore, Keller suggests, not only was McClintock's argument at odds with prevalent theories in mainstream genetics, but also her way of communicating it to the scientific community may have made it seem unacceptable or inaccessible.[53] In McClintock's case, and in many other instances across the disciplines, the absence of social linkages—whether that be due to one's inability to be persuasive, or the inability of one's audience to acknowledge unfamiliar ideas, or a combination of both—results in frustration for the inventor and a delay during which a discovery does not resonate in an intellectual community.

While an absence of the quality of resonance may have ill effects on invention, its presence may enhance inventive possibilities. This has been the case even in creativity in literature, which has traditionally been regarded as a private and mysterious affair. The fruitful association of a group of writers in a given time and place has been chronicled in studies of twentieth century literary figures in Paris who gathered at Sylvia Beach's shop, Shakespeare and Company, or at Gertrude Stein's studio at 27, rue de Fleures. It was evident in England in the group of Bloomsbury writers and, as recently demonstrated by Nicholas Delbanco in *Group Portrait*, in the relationships among five writers living south of London, circa 1900: Joseph Conrad, Stephen Crane, Ford Madox Ford, Henry James, and H. G. Wells. "Whether one calls it a movement or a group," Delbanco says of those whose circle he portrays, "whether one insists on influence or describes it as collegiality, whether the friendships were lasting or transient, this much is irreducible: five major talents worked in close proximity. And the contact was not accidental or occasioned by geography alone." Of their relationship, Delbanco emphasizes that "they aided each other, or tried to, and the aid and comfort helped."[54]

Informal associations that foster literary creativity have existed in America as well. A notable example is the Gotham Book Mart on West 47th Street in Manhattan. Founded by Frances Steloff in 1920, the Gotham has for more than sixty years given avant-garde writers a place to be read and heard as part of a living artistic and intellectual community. In recognition of this work, Steloff received the distinguished service award of the National Institute of Arts and Letters. She has helped writers in many practical ways: organizing readings, holding parties to celebrate new publications, loaning writers money, and advertising their needs. Her catalogues brought news of the avant-garde to many parts of the world. She provided shelf space for known and unknown writers alike and made available the "little" experimental magazines (*transition, Story, View, Horizon*) that were unprofitable for her shop but important in making known new literary work.

The Gotham's basement served as a sanctuary for writers who did not want to leave their books in Europe during World War II for fear they would be destroyed. Writers gave talks at the shop, donating admission proceeds to buy an occasional dinner for a hungry poet. When Henry Miller's books were banned in the United States,

Steloff helped to smuggle them into the country and sell them, though she could have been jailed for doing so. She loaned Anaïs Nin money to buy a printing press on which Nin printed her own works. The Gotham promoted the works of Joyce in America and held meetings that gave rise to the Joyce Society. Often at the Gotham, introductions have been made and letters written that helped writers' careers. The list of writers and other book people associated with Steloff and the Gotham is very long indeed, including (to name but a few) Henry Miller, Marianne Moore, Kay Boyle, Anaïs Nin, Kenneth Patchen, James Dickey, James Laughlin, Edith Sitwell, and Katherine Anne Porter.[55]

Invention requires people who act as Steloff has, whether they be called enablers, resonators, friends, sponsors, liaisons, or brokers of arts and letters. Those who attempt to assist invention by bridging the distance between inventor and audience are scarce indeed, largely because they are worked so hard and paid so little. By insufficiently acknowledging the value of such enablers, we may ultimately be inhibiting creativity. Informal associations between people play a significant role in enabling creative thinking. Perhaps it is misleading to refer to these as part of "social context," if the term implies that such relationships are merely a background in which creative acts of individuals occur. The varied types of collaborations—loose or structured, in pairs or groups, lasting for minutes or years—deserve recognition as an integral part of invention.

Invention and the Social Collective

Writers do not invent in a vacuum. Expectations of society, attitudes fostered by institutions, funding preferences of public and private agencies, tacit rules about the nature of evidence and procedures for inquiry, and availability of equipment and materials— these are but a few examples of what influences our inventions. Forces exerted by social collectives prohibit some inventions and promote others, as these instances suggest:

> Herbert Marcuse, in *One-Dimensional Man*, claims that advanced industrial society is determined by technological progress. In the interest of maintaining that progress, opposition is not permitted. Society finds ways—through language, political structures, and projected attitudes—

to contain any qualitative change that would threaten the technological status quo. Since technology generally provides enough people with enough material benefits, they allow this totalitarian control to continue. According to Marcuse, alternative ideas and true dialectical oppositions cannot even be imagined as possibilities.[56] These are *topoi* to which no one may go.

Prohibition: Do not invent that which contradicts society's goals.

An assistant professor in a department that favors empirical, quantitative studies in communication has published several articles in that vein. She wants to write something very different: something theoretical that may even be seen to question the significance of her previous work. She comes up for tenure in two years and she has been told it is to her advantage to have a coherent body of work that contributes to the mission of her department.

Promotion: Invent what is consistent with what you have previously invented. Invent what is compatible with the inventions of those who judge you. Stay in your own territory.

A doctoral student in engineering comes to his university's writing center for help with his dissertation's conclusions and recommendations. He has ideas about what to say, but his advisor does not want him to write them, since the agency that funded the research may read the report and conclude that the project is essentially completed, in which case they may not renew the grant. No amount of discussion with a tutor about invention as a personal, autonomous act—no talk of freewriting or brainstorming or tagmemics—will solve this invention problem.

Prohibition: Do not invent what may jeopardize the funding that sponsored your invention.

In America, the McCarthy investigations of alleged Communist activites restricted many people from inventing in certain ways and punished those who dared to associate with others who would not abide by the anti-Marxist, anti-Communist dictates. Careers were ruined, books banned, reputations tarnished. In the Soviet Union, a noted researcher, A. R. Luria, had to stop his research programs several times and invent not simply new lines of inquiry but entirely new careers—as a psychologist, a neuropsychologist, then a specialist in mental retardation—because the Soviet government did not approve of what he discovered in his research and prevented him from publishing his findings.

Prohibition: Do not invent what your government does not favor, unless you are prepared to suffer the consequences.

A student is given a choice of topic for a research paper in sociology class. She considers writing about the effects on society if abortion became illegal. She is not sure what she thinks about the matter, but wonders if writing about it might help her decide. A Catholic by birth, she attends a Catholic university. Her professor has not discussed the topic in class, but is rumored to have spoken against a pro-choice position. The student's grade hovers between B and C; she needs a 3.0 to keep her scholarship. What should she say in her paper? Should she even write about that topic?

Promotion: When in doubt, invent the safest way out.

The need to end World War II led to innovation in physics as applied to the development of nuclear weapons. John F. Kennedy's mandate to put an American on the moon before the Russians led to innovation in space technology. Public concern about the high incidence of cancer channeled funds for medical research into cancer research.

Promotion: If you need support, choose a line of inquiry that fits with the goals of public and private institutions. Necessity is the mother of invention.

In the above cases, invention is influenced by a social collective, a supra-individual entity whose rules and conventions may enable or inhibit the invention of certain ideas. Even when an individual appears to invent in isolation or with one or two others, she is also interacting with social collectives. The locus of evaluation of what is invented, according to this perspective, lies in this larger social unit: the organization, institution, bureaucracy, government, political system, tradition, or socioculture.

Theoretical Foundation: Emile Durkheim

A theoretical foundation for this collective view of invention is found in the work of Emile Durkheim. For Durkheim, one explains human behavior by studying the social collective. When individuals live together, orienting their behavior to one another and harmonizing their actions, they give rise to society, a collective unit that is greater than the sum of its individual parts. Society emerges from the interactions of individuals and in turn influences them to act in certain ways.

When one adopts a collective perspective, the important concerns for study are "social facts," ideas that exist in the abstract, collective "mind" of society. People are not always consciously aware of the force that social facts exert on their thoughts and actions, but they are influenced nonetheless.[57] The basic categories that organize human experience—categories such as time, space, class, and number, the "permanent moulds for the mental life"[58]—originate in the social collective and impose themselves on people. These categories are, Durkheim says, "priceless instruments of thought which the human groups have forged through the centuries and where they have accumulated the best of their intellectual capital" (*The Elementary Forms*, p. 19). Durkheim's pattern of study is to look for the cause of human behavior not in innate characteristics or psychological traits, nor in interpersonal relationships, but in the ways individuals are related to the features and forces that come from an over-arching society.

Applying Durkheim's theory to the study of invention brings us to the far end of the continuum, at a considerable distance from the Platonic view that holds that individuals invent by mining what lies within. By contrast, the most extreme version of a collective perspective would stress that invention comes from without: the socioculture itself is what thinks through individuals or by means of individuals. It is as if an idea floats somewhere in the collective waiting for a propitious time and place and person in which it may manifest itself. In contrast to the internal dialogic invention, in which an individual incorporates social influences but can modify them through an internal dialectic, the collective view sees ideas as virtually imposed on individuals from without.

As I noted previously, the theories of creativity of Kroeber and Gray take this extreme view that culture is what actually does the creating. Leslie A. White advocates a similar view, stating that given the existence of certain materials and conditions and interactions, one can conclude that a discovery is bound to occur. For that reason, he claims, it is not surprising when the same idea—one whose time has come—is discovered independently by a number of people at the same time. As examples, White cites the independently made discoveries of sunspots in 1611 by Galileo, Fabricus, Scheiner, and

Harriot, and the understanding of respiration arrived at in 1777 by Priestley, Scheele, Lavoisier, Spallanzani, and Davy (White, in Arieti, p. 301).

Taken less extremely, the collective perspective may be used to look at invention not as an entirely passive act of people who are acted upon by their socioculture, but as an act that is to a considerable extent influenced by forces originating in social collectives. A key way of explaining why something is or is not invented by a particular person would then be to look at the manner in which inventors are attached to a social collective. If, for example, individuals' attachments to social collectives are strong, their ideas may be very much in accord with the prevailing collective views or rules; if their attachments are weak, they may be more likely to produce ideas that are alien to a collective, ones that will face considerable resistance from people who are more firmly attached to collectively held views. Ideas supported by one collective (e.g., the church) may conflict with those held by another overlapping collective (the state).

Adopting a collective view of invention, then, we might look at patterns, trends, or rules originating in a social collective and influencing the inventive powers or processes of individuals or collaborators for better or for worse. Both tacit and explicit rules within a bureaucratic organization or an entire society about what is and is not allowed to be thought or said are relevant to invention considered from this perspective. In contemporary Western culture, for instance, there is a tacit endorsement of innovation: it is *good* to invent something new. Yet according to Marcuse's analysis in *One-Dimensional Man*, not all inventions are created equal, and some are not allowed at all. Through the closing of the universe of discourse, Marcuse tells us, advanced industrialized societies prevent the birth of ideas that would impede technological progress and encourage developments that foster the growth of technology. An increasing awareness of the enormous role that forces beyond the individual play in discoveries may drastically alter our ways of studying and teaching about the process of invention.

Such a collective perspective may at first seem alien. In his discussion of Durkheim's concept of a collective mind that exists beyond individuals, Geoffrey Sampson observes that this notion seems strange and perhaps mystical to us because we are simply more accustomed to thinking of "mind" as entirely individual. Yet there is also a sense of the mystical, Sampson points out, "attached to the notion of an individual mind which is quite different in kind from but intimately related to the particular piece of matter we call a brain; if we can swallow this notion, *perhaps* we should not choke on Durkheim's 'collective mind'" (p. 54).

Still, the average composition teacher will find individual "mind" less startling than an abstract "collective mind" or a "social fact." What is it that we are trying to say about a writer's invention process when we say that at times it is most appropriate to take a collective perspective? Are we, in effect, to tell a writer that he invents by letting the collective think through him? That is perhaps no less extreme, however, than current views suggesting that a writer invents by releasing a mysterious, hidden entity—authentic self, innate structures, true voice, private meaning—that he projects onto an outer world. Which is the greater fiction: the solitary individual existing apart from social collectives or the abstract collective existing over and above individuals? Both fictions show us something about reality. The fiction of the individual has been with us for so long, however, that it is difficult to try the collective fiction on for size, even though it may be instructive, perhaps revealing potential benefits even as it reminds us of the dangers of brainwashing and "group-think."

Take art history, for example. A persistent problem here, Linda Nochlin notes, is that art historians have not taken the trouble to look into "the role that the social order plays" in the nurturing of what is eventually considered to be great art. Questions about what conditions are conducive to the making of great art have been dismissed as being "unscholarly, too broad, or the province of some other discipline like sociology." [59] When one is made to answer the question that is the title of Nochlin's article—"Why Are There No Great Women Artists?"—without looking to social conditions and influences, one is left to concede that the reason must be that women have some innate flaw or lack some significant ingredient necessary to the making of great art. Inventiveness in art, like inventiveness in writing, is traditionally assumed to be released from within: the Great Artist comes, Nochlin announces, "bearing within his person since birth a mysterious essence, rather like the golden nugget in Mrs. Grass's chicken soup, called genius or talent, which

must always out, no matter how unlikely or unpromising the circumstances" (p. 489). From this myth, Nochlin extracts the syllogism that prevails: "if women had the golden nugget of artistic genius, then it would reveal itself. But it has never revealed itself.
Q.E.D. Women do not have the golden nugget of artistic genius"
(p. 491).

Of course, once we stop insisting that the only item of consequence in this issue is whether one possesses—yes or no?—that
golden nugget, we find there are other questions worth asking.
Nochlin poses several: From what social classes or castes have artists
come in different historical periods? How many good artists have
had parents and close relatives who were also artists? Did women
have access to other painters as role models? Did women receive
training? Did the expectations placed upon women in regard to
other work (as mother, hostess, wife) make it unlikely that they
would have the time or energy or concentration necessary to become great artists (pp. 491–93)?

Nochlin's argument illustrates the point that a theoretical perspective on invention that overemphasizes what is innate in an isolated
individual will not afford a full understanding of the complexities involved. The traditional view of women's supposed lack of artistic creativity is part of a more general social "fact" carried for centuries by
the social collective. That is, simply put, that women do not, should
not, indeed cannot, invent—or if they should by some quirk happen to do so, their inventions will be slight and will be restricted to
certain domains. This pervasive social fact is then corroborated by
various perspectives that focus on something innate in the individual: sometimes biology (she lacks a hormone that gives men the
drive to achieve); or sometimes psychology (she needs to help others
and fears success; she resists abstraction, likes particulars, hates
numbers).[60]

A collectivity infuses its institutions with social facts, and then the
institutions, as well as smaller social groups and individuals, opera-
tionalize the dictates. If, for example, it is (or has been) a "social
fact" that women can't invent, then it follows that men needn't allow
women into professional organizations. If women don't have such af-
filiations, they are indeed less likely to invent when they lack the
benefits of membership, such as the chance to work collaboratively,
to present ideas in a forum, to publish, and to seek awards to support research. When women then do *not* invent, the social fact is

confirmed: women can't invent. (We knew it all along.) Such has been the experience for many women in literature and science, to name but two examples. Louise Bernikow lists institutions of literary life that have favored men and ignored women: "'The School of Donne,' 'the tribe of Ben,' 'the Wordsworth Circle,' 'the Rhymers' Club,' 'the Pre-Raphaelite Brotherhood'—in such clusters have the intellectual movements of the past been brought to us."[61] Male poets congregated to share "whatever was to be shared and spread a certain infectious energy among themselves"; women, Bernikow notes, might serve tea and sit in a back room "copying over manuscripts so the work of the men would make marks for posterity."[62] As Margaret Rossiter points out in *Women Scientists in America*, women-only groups convened to discuss scientific matters, but these were not the official organizations. Until the last half of the nineteenth century, women were largely excluded from scientific societies such as the Academy of Natural Science and the American Academy of Arts and Sciences, and thus they were in important ways isolated from mainstream science.[63]

The point of all this is that if we communicate to people, women *or* men, in ever so many ways the message that they can't create in literature, art, science, or any other field, and if we separate them from other people and institutions that might foster creativity, then we shouldn't be surprised if they do not invent. We should in fact be surprised when, despite all odds, they do. Encouraging inventors to look exclusively within, as if they can always solve the problem themselves, may divert attention from the main problem and preserve the status quo. What Linda Nochlin insists that those who are concerned with art must realize applies equally to those of us concerned with invention in any sphere: we must insist that the making of art (or science or philosophy or any field) "both in terms of the development of the art maker and the nature and quality of the work of art itself, occurs in a social situation, is an integral element of the social structure, and is mediated and determined by specific and definable social institutions, be they art academics, systems of patronage, mythologies of the divine creator and artist as he-man or social outcast" (p. 493).

Examples of Modern Collective Perspectives

The idea that a collective force permeates a society and acts (often through established institutions and conventions) to influence the attitudes and behavior and inventions of members of social groups is found in the work of theorists in various fields. As examples, let us consider theorists concerned with language and with science.

Certain linguists have favored a view of language itself as a collective force which, by virtue of its vocabulary and syntax, may influence how its speakers perceive and think about reality. This force would clearly affect what language-thinkers invent. The Sapir-Whorf view of language as a shaper of thought is an obvious example. "Every language and every well-knit technical sublanguage," Whorf maintains, "incorporates certain points of view and certain patterned resistances to widely divergent points of view."[64] Adam Schaff's philosophy of language, while avoiding the extreme implications of the Whorfian view of linguistic relativity, maintains nevertheless that "every language includes a definite *Weltanschauung*, a definite schema or stereotype of the way in which the world of things and events is perceived."[65] The idea of language as a collective foundation of society makes more sense, Schaff claims, than mystical notions of a 'spirit of the nation' or a 'national vital force' that are attempts at vaguely accounting for influence of society on individuals."[66]

To understand the nature of language, theorists such as Ferdinand de Saussure and Hilary Putnam have taken what amounts to a collective perspective. As Durkheim focuses on the social collective rather than the individual to study human behavior, so Saussure concentrates on *langue*, the collective, abstract system of language, as opposed to *parole*, language produced by the individual speaker. Similarly, Putnam regards semantics as best understood in a communal rather than an individual sense. The meanings of words, he says (with Wittgenstein), do not reside in individual minds; rather, meaning arises from the use of words according to social rules in a community (Putnam in Sampson, pp. 45–46).

The preference of a linguist (or any other theorist) for one approach over another—for a collective rather than a Platonic view, say—may in turn be culturally or collectively influenced. For instance, in discussing the contrast between Saussure's focus on language as a social fact of the collectivity and Chomsky's focus on the idiolect of the individual, Geoffrey Sampson observes that each theorist may have been culturally influenced to adopt his view. The French tendency to standarize and maintain the purity of language as a whole may have reinforced Saussure's concentration on the abstract system of language, while English-speaking societies, less concerned with "language-canonizing institutions," may have favored a Chomskian concentration on the individual. "The pattern of a scholar's thought," Sampson goes on to say, "will often be influenced by presuppositions current in his intellectual milieu even though they involve beliefs which he would reject if he confronted them explicitly" (p. 55).

Adherence to such tacit ideas and attitudes may constitute what James L. Adams calls "cultural blocks" to creativity, which in Western culture include notions that humor is out of place in problem-solving; that tradition is preferable to change; that reason, logic, and numbers are features of "right-handed thinking," which is good; that intuition and qualitative judgments involving sensitivity and subjectivity are features of "left-handed thinking," which is bad. Cultural blocks are maintained and furthered by institutional practices. Agencies that fund scientific research, Adams notes, favor proposals that are based on right-handed thinking, since the decision-makers are themselves influenced by the cultural block against left-handed thinking in science, and since they must answer to others who hold the same bias. "Many of the soft sciences," Adams claims, "have sought to become more quantitative and rigorous in order to take better advantage of our cultural bias toward right-handed thinking." [67]

Where a view prevails of science as an entirely rational, objective enterprise in which people pursue incontestable truths about what exists "out there" in a physical world that is separable from its human observers, one would not expect a social collectivity to have much to do with the growth of scientific knowledge. Recent views advanced by rhetoricians and philosophers of science, however, emphasize science as a social enterprise in which knowledge evolves by means of argument in a community that accepts or rejects certain problems, concepts, procedures, and kinds of evidence. Whether or not something is accepted as scientific "truth" has a great deal to do with how its case is argued in the community of scientists. Received beliefs, which are collectively acknowledged in scientific communities, form the conceptual foundation for invention in science. They give support to compatible new ideas and resistance to ideas that differ and must be tested against the existing body of knowledge. Thomas Kuhn has been much quoted in his use of the term "paradigms" to refer to "accepted examples of actual scientific practice—examples which include law, theory, application, and instrumentation together." Paradigms are models that give rise to scientific research, Kuhn says; and new discoveries, when they are (often with much controversy) accepted by the scientific community, may cause the basic conceptual paradigms to shift.[68]

Another concept of a collective body of knowledge and practice in science, one which predates and is in some ways similar to Kuhn's, is evident in Ludwik Fleck's view of a "thought collective," which he develops in his study of the way the medical community evolved its diagnosis and treatment of syphilis. Knowledge, for Fleck, is carried by a "thought collective," a "community of persons exchanging ideas or maintaining intellectual interaction"; the thought collective is itself a carrier of the "prevailing thought style," a readiness to perceive and assimilate things in a certain way, which determines the way knowledge in the field will develop.[69] The power of the thought collective is similar to that of Durkheim's social collective. The social realm is of paramount importance in science for Fleck: "Cognition is the most socially-conditioned activity of man," Fleck notes, "and knowledge is the paramount social creation. The very structure of language presents a compelling philosophy characteristic of that community." (p. 42). For Fleck, cognition involves not only the relationship between subject and object, but also the relationship with a third, collective entity: the existing fund of knowledge contained in the thought collective. The individual is largely unaware of the prevailing thought style of a collective, but it "almost always exerts an absolutely compulsive force upon his thinking" (p. 41). While individuals do play an important role in discovery, Fleck admits, in much of science and medicine, the individual who is identified as discoverer is part of a team, building on a fund of collectively held knowledge, and is "rather a standard-bearer in discovery than its sole agent" (p. 42). According to this view of scientific discovery, it is essential to investigate the social collective as well as the individual to understand the development and acceptance of knowledge.

Collectives as Aids to Invention

The examples I have given to show the influence of collectives on invention—Marcuse's view of the closing of the universe of discourse; the exclusion of women from professional status in literature and science; the "cultural blocks" Adams sees restricting creativity—may imply that the collective serves chiefly to inhibit invention. It is indeed true that collectives exert forces that bias perception and cognition, and cause resistance to styles of thought or types of evidence that differ from those they espouse. However, the collective can be a positive as well as a restrictive force, aiding invention by providing structures for thinking and for creating and evaluating new ideas. In *The Scientific Imagination*, Gerald Holton conceives of scientific discovery as involving empirical, logical, and thematic dimensions. Themata, which are generally held, tacit concepts originating from both individual efforts and historical developments, often occur as antithetical pairs such as atomism/continuum or hierarchy/unity: "The deep attachment of some scientists to certain over-arching themata," Holton explains, "may well be one of the chief sources of innovative energy."[70] Such concepts of antitheses recognized by an intellectual community may provide direction and energy, thus acting as an impetus for new ideas.

Collective forces may influence invention when we least expect it. Even in the case of Freud's work, for example, which seems very much to be the invention of an individual man about individual men, collective forces likely provided both encouragement and resistance. To understand Freud's discoveries and process of invention, Harold Lasswell has said, it is necessary to look not only to subjective events that may have occurred in Freud's mind, but also to the social setting with which these subjective events must have interacted. As Lasswell explains, "one does not overlook the exposure to Jewish culture during formative years (modified by the presence of a by now famous Catholic nurse); or the fact that Freud's family setting was middle class, with characteristic demands to rise in the world; or the influence of the special interests of a neurologist and physician provided with opportunity to study hypnotic supplements to chemical, physical, and other currently standard models of therapy" (p. 211).

Innovation is much more likely to occur, Lasswell notes, when a person is expected to do something constructive and when he expects that of himself. Although Freud's discoveries were eventually criticized in Vienna and elsewhere, his cultural heritage and social setting likely encouraged him to make discoveries of some sort.

"Vienna was a great creative center of culture, notably in medicine," Lasswell explains. "The personnel of the university, and especially of the faculty of medicine, was under the pressure of the environment (including one another) to add to scientific and medical knowledge. From the earliest days of student competition the accepted goal was defined broadly in such challenging terms" (p. 212). Viewed in these terms, Freud's invention in psychology is understood, at least in part, as a socially influenced act.

Shifts in values and needs of social collectives may also incline a society toward promotion of certain kinds of innovations (Lasswell, p. 214). During World War II, for example, innovations in weapon design and manufacture, most prominently the development of the atomic bomb, were fostered by social pressures to win the war. In recent years, American public and private institutions have greatly increased financial support for cancer research, an area little investigated in the past. Invention in any field is a continuous process of problem-finding and problem-solving. Individuals are more likely to think creatively, Lasswell points out, if they have inherited a map that has the potential to generate many new ideas, a map they may labor to fill in (p. 213). Lasswell's case in point is Einstein's contribution to other scientific innovators:

> Mathematical physicists who came after Einstein were exposed to a preliminary version of the natural order that transformed the direction of science. I recall a seminar at the University of Berlin that included Einstein and Von Neumann, then in his twenties. Einstein would sometimes put an equation on the board and presently get tangled up. Von Neumann would go to the board and with great virtuosity put things in order. I recall the remark of a participant, 'Of course Einstein is partly pre-Einsteinian; young Von Neumann has the good luck to be Einsteinian from the beginning'. (pp. 213–14).

Inventors in any sphere are fortunate if they inherit good problems that serve as an impetus for invention. In mathematics, for instance, Paul Halmos has said that a major challenge is finding key problems. Mathematicians in this century have profited, he claims, because they inherited a list containing "23 searching questions put together by David Hilbert and presented at the International Congress of Mathematicians in Paris in 1900."[71] Such a declaration may be absorbed by a field and may constitute a mandate for research, thus influencing the direction of creative thought for some time, for better or for worse. If the mandate is adopted as a basis for decision-making in awarding grants for research, it may be extremely influential in regard to the kinds of questions that will be asked or unasked as well as the methods and assumptions by which research will proceed.

Even in literature, which many regard as an asocial enterprise, collectively held knowledge and styles of thinking influence invention. Having a common heritage of creative thinkers and writers, and knowing about that heritage, can be a source of creativity for individual writers. Even if one is unaware of such collective influence, Virginia Woolf suggests, it is nonetheless operating. Had not one woman, and then another, and yet another come to have a habit of writing, so that it gradually became less bizarre to think that women *could* create in writing, then the act of a single would-be woman writer would scarcely have been possible. "For masterpieces are not single and solitary births," Woolf says. "They are the outcome of many years of thinking in common, of thinking by the body of the people, so that the experience of the mass is behind the single voice."[72] Collective experience thus gives substance and validity to what a writer writes. And again: "I am talking of the common life which is the real life and not of the little separate lives which we live as individuals."[73] Woolf's "we" is the collectivity of all women writers; it is necessary, she believes, for women to think of themselves in a collective sense, with their shared characteristics and restrictions and circumstances, if they are to understand their status as writers and creative thinkers.

Nor is a collective heritage for women only. T. S. Eliot's noted 1919 essay about poetry claims that individual talent must necessarily be influenced by tradition and that tradition itself is altered by the supervention of new work by new writers. Eliot's "tradition" is a kind of collective entity: it is a shared sense that emerges from individual writers and their works, and it is more than the sum of its parts. Tradition is carried by a collective mind, "the mind of Europe—the mind of his [the poet's] own country—a mind which he learns in time to be much more important than his own private mind."[74] An individual who writes with an understanding of tradition does not simply imitate his predecessors. Instead, Eliot ex-

plains, one writes from a historical sense that "involves a perception, not only of the pastness of the past, but of its presence" and
that "compels a man to write not only with his own generation in his
bones, but with a feeling that the whole of the literature of Europe
from Homer and within it the whole of his own country has a simultaneous existence and imposes a simultaneous order" (p. 603). The
poet's understanding of those whose work has come before him must
infuse and inform his sense of the present if his work is to be truly
excellent. To be fully individual, we might say, one must be infused
with his social heritage.

Furthermore, an individual must be judged by and in relation to
other people who have created before: "You cannot value him alone;
you must set him, for contrast and comparison, among the dead. I
mean this as a principle of aesthetic, not merely historical criticism"
(p. 603). The creation of good art and literature, then, requires both
inventor and audience to have a sense of the collective body of inventions that has come before. This collective of tradition is, to
Eliot, not an encumbrance but an essential source of invention and
judgment. In any sphere of invention, individuals and groups must
find ways of to think with, and through, and contrary to the collective body of ideas and ways of thinking which both enable and restrict people. "Creativity is not an escape from culture," Stephen
Jay Gould has said, "but a unique use of its opportunities combined
with a clever end run around its constraints."[75]

Conclusion

In discussing the first three perspectives on rhetorical invention—the Platonic, internal dialogic, and collaborative views—I
have been able to point to composition theorists and textbooks that
are based on one or more of the views. The Platonic and internal
dialogic views have predominated in the teaching of composition
since the nineteenth century, while recent trends have fostered the
interactive type of collaborative invention in which others help an
individual writer to invent. Of invention brought about through
coauthorship, or invention by more than one person in constrained
circumstances such as negotiations, little is heard in the composition classroom. Seldom discussed, I imagine, is the notion that social relationships may help or hinder inventors by enabling or not

allowing their ideas to resonate—to be received and extended by others.

Perhaps the most telling point that becomes evident in applying this continuum to inventional theories is that almost no composition theorist emphasizes or indeed even alludes to the need for a collective view of invention. Even though the force of collectives looms large in the twentieth century, we find this matter largely unaddressed in contemporary composition. Perhaps the force of collectives on invention is, like many a social fact, taken so much for granted that it passes unnoticed and unarticulated, even as it is omnipresent. Paying greater attention to the collective view of invention may help us take advantage of the positive roles of collectives and beware of unquestioning acquiescence to controls or limits placed on thought and invention.

A theoretical continuum that includes various social perspectives on invention asks us to look at the inventing writer as part of a community, a socioculture, a sphere of overlapping (and sometimes conflicting) collectives. It draws our attention to social contexts, discourse communities, political aims. It reminds us that writers invent not only in the study but also in the smoke-filled chamber; not only alone but with others with whom they must work, or with whom they choose to think; and not in utter isolation even when they are alone, but by means of inner conversations carried on with internalized others. One invents in part because of others, because one thinks fruitfully in the company of a great many others, who are both possible and real.

In 1970, the Committee on the Nature of Rhetorical Invention of the Speech Communication Association recommended that rhetoricians seek a scheme with which to examine the process of rhetorical invention, one that could be a "generative theory of rhetoric." The report suggests four criteria for judging such a scheme, and these criteria are, I hope, at least partially satisfied by the continuum I have proposed here. This scheme, they say, should do the following: (1) accommodate not just specific topics, but entire systems of invention; (2) allow interplay among those inventional systems; (3) provide "a marketplace of ideas in competition" to allow analysis and comparison of different views to be freely considered and debated; and (4) treat the systems according to their functional value in the process of invention.[76]

The continuum I have proposed allows for treatment of entire systems of invention; included, for example, in this discussion are various conceptions of the inventing writer, from the prewriting perspective to the conceptual theory of rhetoric to tagmemic invention. The continuum also fulfills the second requirement to allow for overlap and interplay of systems of invention. One might think of invention in some cases as moving from a writer's dialogue with an internalized other to a collaborative process of inventing with peers in an organization, all the while influenced by the collective force of the organization's goals and the culture's prohibitions and expectations. This continuum also allows one system of invention to be examined from its various perspectives; we may, for instance, see both Platonic and internal dialogic elements in tagmemic invention. The third criterion—provision for competitive ideas—is met in that the traditional Platonic view of invention is given its place along with other perspectives that admit varying kinds and degrees of social involvement in invention. And to satisfy the fourth criterion, that the functional value of inventional systems receive emphasis, I have illustrated the working of the theories in practice with examples from a variety of writing situations in occupations as well as classrooms, along with examples of various pedagogical methods used by composition teachers.

Applying this continuum to existing inventional theories allows us to see that composition has favored Platonic and internal dialogic views of invention, and that while the field has begun to acknowledge some collaborative aspects of invention, it has neglected others and has virtually ignored a collective view. The collaborative and collective perspectives help us not so much to understand existing ways of thinking and teaching about invention as to ask how they might be reconceptualized, expanded, or otherwise altered. In the last chapter I will discuss the implications of these findings, but I think it is evident at this point that to continue to neglect the ways inventors collaborate and the ways collectives help or hinder invention would be to settle for a limited view—an unfinished sketch, a look through a jammed kaleidoscope—of what happens when writers invent. Taking a social perspective should bring our picture into sharper focus.

5

The Role of Language:
A Foundation for
a Social Perspective
on Invention

Language and Rhetorical Invention

Whenever we think and write about language, which is itself so much a part of our thinking, a degree of uncertainty seems unavoidable. Such self-conscious reflection in language about language is, George Steiner advises, "a proceeding inside a circle of mirrors" that necessarily invites counterstatement: "Each statement, if it is to be of any serious interest at all, will be another way of asking." [1]

In this chapter I am concerned with a "way of asking" two main questions that explore language as a foundation for a view of invention as a social act. First: is it appropriate to regard language as an active force in thinking and inventing rather than a passive copy of the "real thing," whether that be an external object or an internal thought? And second: to what extent should we consider the use of language in invention to be a social act relying on a shared system of symbols developed and used by a language community, as opposed to the private act of individuals?

To explore these questions, I will draw on pertinent insights from various linguists, psychologists, and philosophers of language to suggest that we re-examine some prevalent assumptions about language, especially as it relates to invention. I review copy theory as it pertains to language and to the relationship between knowledge and reality. I then discuss Immanuel Kant's advance over copy theory and Ernst Cassirer's extension of Kant's philosophy to include symbolization and the role of culture in influencing the ways we constitute reality. This movement in the philosophy of language away from copy theory toward symbolic forms provides a theoretical basis for understanding the role of language in a view of invention as a social act. I ask that we give serious consideration to two main conclusions. First, language should be viewed as an active force in the way we constitute—not simply *copy*—reality; language thus plays an active role in how we perceive and think and invent. Second, language should be viewed in its development and its use as a dialectic between individual and social realms. Invention that occurs with language has often been understood as a principally intrapsychic event that goes on privately within the individual. Yet language is inevitably social as well. It is what we inherit from previous generations, what we learn from others, what we share with others. Language, which is to a considerable extent the basis for invention, is thus itself the result of an ongoing social process.

Traditionally, those concerned with what have been called (misleadingly, no doubt) "creative" or "literary" uses of language have been likely to favor the first conclusion and oppose the second; that is, they would affirm the active role that language plays in creating a world (albeit a fictitious world rather than the one we live in day-to-day), but they would emphasize that this creation is an individual rather than a social act. On the other hand, those concerned mainly with scientific or technical writing or with what has been called "functional" writing—writing in which the "real world" supposedly does its work—tend to de-emphasize the creative role of language or to regard it as an obstacle to a clear rendering of the world as it exists objectively. At the same time, they affirm the social over the individual aspect of language, social in that it stresses a common understanding of a world we all share, as opposed to a private or fictitious world that an individual might create.

Fortunately, writers and teachers are becoming increasingly aware that these differences between aspects or uses of language are not as extreme as they are often made to seem, though textbooks continue either to avoid discussions of the nature and uses of language, or to make statements about language that are unhelpful or even misleading. The viewpoints I advocate here should, I think, be acceptable to both the literary and the functional language "camps" if they keep in mind that each is interested in emphasizing, perhaps exploiting, different aspects of the full range of possibilities that language offers, and that the differences are not always as great as they are automatically assumed to be. A dogmatic, simplified view of language leads us to underestimate the role that language plays in invention and indeed in inquiry. I suggest that the two points I will stress about language and its relationship to invention—first, language as an active force in the ways we constitute reality and invent material for discourse, and second, invention with language as a dialectic between individual and social realms—should be a part of the education of all writers, whether they be scientists, engineers, historians, novelists, or technical writers.

Words: The Curtain over the Windowpane

Just as rhetorical invention has been thought of as either dynamic or reflective, so has language been alternately approached as either an active or passive entity. A view of language as dynamic and creative is put forth, for example, by William Gass, in his philosophical essay on language, *On Being Blue*. Gass emphasizes the power of language and the symbolic world over physical things, claiming that a writer "should give up the blue things of this world in favor of the words which say them."[2] Less extreme than Gass is Ernst Cassirer, who is nevertheless a strong advocate of the active role that language plays. Language, Cassirer claims, does not merely copy an external world; rather, as we use language in our social environment, we in a sense "invent" the reality we will deal with, on the basis of shared rules that are firmly grounded in society. Only when we name the "chaos of immediate impressions" does it take on order and become clear for us.[3]

But before we consider more fully the view of language as an active and constitutive force, we should review the opposite argument, one that has commanded much attention in the past and continues to permeate the assumptions behind much teaching about scientific and technical writing. This view of language as passive holds that language is a copy of some other, extralinguistic reality.

That reality—which is assumed to be the legitimate one—may be located in an external world of objects or an internal world of thought. In either case, language becomes a partial representation, a reproduction or copy, a second class citizen in someone else's country. The work of language according to this view is to reflect, often inadequately or incompletely or downright misleadingly, something that is outside itself.

"Tell it like it is" would be a popular culture way of saying what language tries to do, and "like" would be an important word here since it implies that language is an analogy for what really exists. People have for some time desired a language that would copy external reality perfectly. In his *Essay on Man*, Cassirer mentions the dream people have had of recovering a *lingua Adamica*, a lost universal language, "a 'real' language of the first ancestors of man, a language which did not consist merely of conventional signs but which expressed rather the very nature and essence of things."[4] As knowledge grew and as Latin declined from general use in the seventeenth and early eighteenth centuries, the longing for what George Steiner calls "an unambiguous, universal concordance between words and things" led to a movement for a universal language or interlingua that would be a set of symbols for the discovery as well as the expression of all knowledge, useful for international exchange of ideas.[5]

Francis Bacon and John Amos Comenius are cited by Steiner as seventeenth century advocates of a systematic correspondence of word to thing as a way of curing the disorder that has persisted in language ever since Adam's time, when each thing in the garden had its name. Clear thought depends on careful induction from things, Bacon claims in his *Novum Organum* (1620): "The syllogism consists of propositions, propositions of words; words are the signs of notions. If, therefore, the notions (which form the basis of the whole) be confused and carelessly abstracted from things, there is no solidity in the superstructure."[6] John Amos Comenius made this word/thing correspondence explicit in his illustrated textbook for children, *Orbis Pictus*, translated as the *Visible World: or, A Nomenclature, and Pictures of All the Chief Things that are in the World, and of Mens Employment Therein*. Published in 1657 in Nuremberg and translated soon after into English, the text provides a picture for every word, with each word appearing in both English and Latin in a manner so that "every where one word answereth to the word over against it . . . as a man clad in a double garment."[7] We will see other instances of similar metaphors used in copy theories of language: language as a garment, a cloak, a veil, a curtain over the windowpane. Presumably the "real thing"—the extralinguistic meaning—lies concealed beneath or behind these coverings.

Things are all-important to Comenius: ideas, for him, begin in things that are received by the outward senses and converted by the inward senses. His British contemporary Hobbes would likely have approved Comenius's belief that "there is nothing in the understanding which was not before in the sense" (p. xiv). Things are likewise of importance to Thomas Sprat who, ten years after the *Orbis Pictus*, published the *History of the Royal Society* in England. Language, for Sprat and for others reacting against a prevalent ornate style, is always trying to catch up with the physical world of things, trying to achieve the supposed ideal of matching that world. Sprat's goal, often quoted, is "to return back to the primitive purity and shortness, when men deliver'd so many things, almost in an equal number of words."[8] Here the thing exists independently, apart from any human perceiver or inventor.

Again and again, language has been considered to be a problem, a phenomenon that obscures true knowledge. Empiricist views did not subscribe to any natural correspondence between word and thing, but nevertheless continued to give language a bad name. For John Locke, another member of the Royal Society, words are properly considered to be a "medium"—often one of "obscurity and disorder"—interposed between our understanding and the world of "visible objects." [9] For philosopher George Berkeley, words are useful in joining the experience of many people from the past and from many places to be possessed by one person. But according to Berkeley's sensationalist view, Cassirer tells us, reality is concrete and is determined by individuals according to sensory experiences. Language distorts reality, and philosophy must be based on a critique of language to dispel illusion: "Most parts of knowledge have been so strangely perplexed and darkened by the abuse of words and general ways of speech wherein they are delivered," Berkeley claims, "that it may almost be made a question whether language has contributed more to the hindrance or advancement of the sciences. . . . We need only draw the curtain of words to behold the fairest tree of knowledge, whose fruit is excellent, and within the reach of our hand."[10]

How can we draw this "curtain of words"? Such a metaphor implies that it would be ideal if we could simply get rid of language and go straight to the real thing. But even those who are skeptical about the value of language would probably go along with the fictional Jake Horner, a prescriptive grammar teacher in John Barth's *End of the Road*, who says that "Assigning names to things is like assigning roles to people: it is necessarily a distortion, but it is a necessary distortion if one would get on with the plot."[11] If we can't get rid of language, some say, we can at least follow Orwell's advice to make prose as innocuous as possible, like a windowpane; indeed, this has long been a supposed ideal of technical writing in particular.[12] Or we might, on the other hand, try to systematize and simplify language, to reduce its connotations: we might seek a universal code. Hence Comenius's attempt to name and illustrate the visible world, and hence the call of many a scientist and philosopher (Descartes, Delgarno, Wilkins, Leibniz) to seek a universal language.

But the search for a uniform solution seems destined to fail. People live in a variety of social worlds, with different activities uniting each group, and language depends not merely on things but on orientation to social purposes and contexts. The fact that words and things do not have a natural correspondence, Steiner notes, is not a deficit in language: "It is because the correspondence between words and 'things' is, in the logician's sense of the term, 'weak,' that language is strong," Steiner explains. "Reverse these concepts, as artificial universal languages do, and the absence of any natural, complex strength in the ensuing mode of communication is obvious. What Esperanto or Novial does is to translate 'from the top.' Only the more generalized, inert aspects of significance survive" (p. 204). Those who would seek universal concordance between words and things fixed in a universal language would deny language the very flexibility that allows us to embody and create new thoughts. In fact, as we will see more fully in Cassirer, it is the fact that language need *not* remain tied to things that allows it to become symbolic. And with its symbolic power, language begins the move toward abstraction that paves the way for scientific thinking.

Language and Thought

So far we have been concerned with a view of language as a copy of an objective reality which is itself extralinguistic. Sometimes this copy theory is reversed to apply to an internal reality. With this view, language is thought to be a copy of inner thought or pure ideas, which may or may not occur in linguistic form. Language is what we use to capture thought and report results. Ideally, language would correspond perfectly to the ideas it is supposed to reproduce. "Like three impressions of the same seal," says Antoine Lavoisier," the words ought to produce the idea, and the idea to be a picture of the fact." [13] But many would say that this ideal—if it is, indeed, ideal at all—is not attained.

Linguists, psychologists, and philosophers of language continue to debate the extent to which thinking occurs in language as opposed to some nonlinguistic form that language then attempts to copy. This issue is important here since it has implications for understanding the role of language in invention. If invention begins prior to or apart from language—if we think something in a nonlinguistic form and then copy it in words—then language simply reflects that which has already been invented. In that case, words might be regarded, as we have previously seen, as the garb or veil that could obscure or distort what has been invented.

Such a mimetic view of language exists, John Clifford claims, in recent work in cognitive psychology concerning composition: "Cognitivists consistently downplay the potential of language," he notes. "Flower and Hayes, for example, in their problem-solving strategies rely on a mimetic conception of language, one in which words are the cloth of thought, where a writer first knows the subject and then searches for appropriate language." [14] Similar assumptions appear to be made by D. Gordon Rohman and Albert Wlecke, whose 1964 report on prewriting research says that the student "must, first of all, discover that single compelling insight, that 'seed idea,' that organizing concept which will then 'grow into' language. . . . Good statement comes only from the mind's actualization of its urgent content into words on a page." [15] Ideas first, words second, writing third.

Mimetic views of language also linger in many professional and technical writing textbooks and articles, which tend to present language as a medium for reporting what is already known rather than as an accomplice or even an initiator of discovery. One article for teachers, for instance, tells us robustly that "the real guts of business writing" is "intelligent content": "The discipline of translating thoughts *into words* and organizing these thoughts logically has no equal as intellectual training" (emphasis throughout this paragraph is mine).[16] And from a book called *The Science of Scientific Writing*, we learn that "The end result of this process of organizing is that when you sit down *to put your ideas into words*, you only have to think about one bit of your paper at a time."[17] The metalanguage in these instances implies that language is simply a vehicle through which finished thought passes.[18]

The significance of language for thought has also been minimized by the Piagetian influence on developmental psychology. Piaget does not deny that language influences intellectual development in children, but neither does he believe that language is necessary for all thinking. He describes "autistic thought," a mode of thinking that seems chiefly to satisfy an individual's desires, as thinking that occurs mainly in images and is incommunicable through language.[19] Piaget sees certain intellectual operations in use before a child has learned to speak. Moreover, he claims, experiments show that children do not learn to think logically by acquiring words (which would presumably be necessary if thinking is linguistic); rather, they imitate and perform actions to develop logical thought, thus forming concepts from something other than words.[20]

Building on Piaget's work, Hans Furth has carried out research with deaf children and adolescents leading him to agree with Piaget's view that while language assists certain conceptual learning tasks, especially in the reasoning characteristic of formal operations, language is not a necessary precondition for the beginning of formal operations. Furth maintains that the assumption that language is necessary for intelligence and thought has led people to underestimate the learning abilities of deaf people and to educate them in an inappropriate manner. The results of a series of studies that present deaf and hearing children and adolescents with thinking tasks have led Furth to conclude that language is not necessary for developing a capacity for generalizing and abstracting; deaf children who knew little English still performed as well as those with hearing on Furth's tests for concepts of similarity and symmetry.[21]

From many directions, then—linguistics, cognitive and develop-

mental psychology, composition theory, technical writing pedagogy—comes evidence of assumptions that language is not coex-
tensive with thinking, that people are not dependent primarily on
language for what and how they think. The idea that some thinking
may be nonverbal also receives support from introspective reports
of certain artists and scientists. Albert Einstein is often cited as a
representative of this view: "The words or the language, as they are
written or spoken, do not seem to play any role in my mechanism of
thought," Einstein said. "The psychical entities which seem to
serve as elements in thought are certain signs and more or less clear
images. . . . [These elements] are, in my case, of visual and some of
muscular type. Conventional words or other signs have to be sought
for laboriously only in a secondary stage."[22] Michael Faraday, too,
separates language from scientific thought. His *Experimental Researches in Electricity* (1844) names and defines a number of new
terms in order to avoid ambiguity, yet he promises to use them only
when necessary, "for I am fully aware that names are one thing and
science another."[23] We hear echoes of Faraday in physicist A. B.
Arons' 1983 claim that a scientifically literate person should be able
to comprehend "that a scientific concept involves an idea first and a
name afterward, and that understanding does not reside in the technical terms themselves."[24]

    Yet there are many—rhetoricians, scientists, philosophers, lin-
guists, and others—who place a much greater emphasis on the importance of language in thought. For instance, in the preface to his
Elements of Chemistry (1789), Antoine Lavoisier quotes Abbe de
Condillac's maxims on language, which Lavoisier himself supports;
among them, "We think only through the medium of words" and
"The art of reasoning is nothing more than a language well arranged."[25] In contrast to Faraday's "names are one thing and science
is another," Lavoisier argues that it is impossible to separate nomenclature from science; the two are necessarily combined: "We cannot
improve the language without at the same time improving the science itself; neither can we, on the other hand, improve a science
without improving the language or nomenclature which belongs to
it."[26] M. P. Crosland, in his book on the language of chemistry,
quotes Lavoisier's early (1777) references to what was eventually to
be called oxygen: "*pure air*, the best and most respirable part of the
air . . . more air than ordinary air."[27] For this redundant and im-

precise terminology, Crosland tells us, Lavoisier was ridiculed in his time; "for us," Crosland concludes, "it is an indication of the inadequacy of ordinary language on the frontiers of knowledge."[28] Yes: "more air than ordinary air" was clumsy. But Crosland and others who hold such an opinion overlook the valuable contribution that such language makes to scientific discovery. Expressing his ideas helped Lavoisier to isolate a part of air and to think of it as something different, something deserving another name. His verbal distinction between "ordinary" and "pure" air is what brought him to oxygen. Rather than criticize the original language, we might instead praise its enabling function, much as Lavoisier himself has done.

For Ernst Cassirer, whose theories I will later discuss in more detail, there *is* thinking without words, but such thought is confined to the particulars of the here and now. Language, for Cassirer, is "the mighty and indispensable vehicle of thought—a kind of flywheel that carries thought along with its own increasing momentum."[29] The idea that thought is heavily influenced by social speech is important to the work of twentieth century Soviet psychologists such as Vygotsky and Luria. Social speech becomes differentiated within the individual, becoming the inner speech in which a person does much of his thinking. For Vygotsky, an individual is capable of some thought before he speaks, but thought and speech become closely connected in the child at approximately age two, when he begins to discover the symbolic form of language and uses it for intellectual as well as social and affective purposes. "At this point," Vygotsky says, "the knot is tied for the problem of thought and language."[30] In the course of human development, Vygotsky believes, thinking becomes linguistic.

Adam Schaff, whose work is influenced by Marx, Vygotsky, and Luria, strongly advocates the view that thinking is linguistic: "Thinking is always thinking in some language."[31] For Schaff, thought and language are not identical, but they are inextricably intertwined and interdependent. What we call human thinking happens in language, because of language; language is not the outward garb of thought. This monistic view of thought and language is similar to that of Marx, whom Schaff quotes as saying "Language is the immediate actuality of thought" (Marx, in Schaff, p. 102). Schaff defines thinking essentially as what happens when people solve problems, and his definition of language is a broad one that includes use of a system of signs that need not be phonic. If we follow Schaff and think of language as encompassing other symbol systems such as American sign language, we might discover a weakness, or at least an omission, in Furth's conclusions about language and thinking based on his studies of deaf people. Reports of at least two of Furth's studies do not say whether the deaf adolescents in the sample groups used sign language, which Furth himself regards as a linguistic system. Most deaf adolescents in the United States do know sign language, Furth claims. But he does not address the point that knowing sign language could figure in their ability to perform thinking tasks, since it allows them to symbolize and to think with their symbols. If the children in his study knew sign language, then Furth's conclusion that language is not necessary for thinking may not be warranted by his evidence. [32]

Another argument often raised to refute the importance of language to thought is, as we saw earlier, the view that scientists and mathematicians think in nonlinguistic form. Schaff opposes this view, claiming that language has to be involved in discovery processes. He argues, for example, that mathematician B. L. Van der Waerden comes to the wrong conclusion in claiming that Pascal first thought of a curve and used language only afterward to name it. Pascal's process must have involved reasoning, Schaff notes, and reasoning is linguistically based. Furthermore, research itself takes place when a problem is raised, which likely occurs in linguistic terms; and sensory perception and articulation of the physical world require mental and linguistic abstraction based on conceptual schemata. Sensory operations that function in scientific observations do not passively receive data but are involved with language in the choice of what to observe, what to omit, and how to classify (Schaff, pp. 108–10).

The powerful role that language plays in thinking is furthermore stressed in the Sapir-Whorf hypothesis. Edward Sapir has said that language tyrannically structures our expectations, which we project onto the field of experience: "Such categories as number, gender, case, tense . . . are not so much discovered in experience as imposed on it because of the tyrannical hold that linguistic form has upon our orientation in the world." [33] According to this view, language is neither a copy of an inner reality nor a vehicle conveying the results of thought; rather, language virtually dictates what can be thought.

While some would not go so far as to say that we are prisoners of language, contemporary philosophers have tended to counter past, absolutist views of language as an obstacle to thought or an objective mirror of a separate inner or outer reality. Instead, as Chaim Perelman tells us, current views acknowledge the "theses implicit in the language": "Contemporary philosophies . . . have not only recognized the role of language as an indispensable instrument of philosophical communication, but have understood that the choice of a linguistic form is neither purely arbitrary nor simply a carbon copy of reality. The reasons that induce us to prefer one conception of experience, one analogy, to another, are a function of our vision of the world. The form is not separable from the content; language is not a veil which one need only discard or render transparent in order to perceive the real as such; it is inextricably bound up with a point of view, with the taking of a position."[34] With such a view, language becomes not only rhetorical but also epistemic. Language becomes a way of knowing.

Kant and Cassirer: From Copy Theory to Symbolic Forms

The relationships of word to thing and of language to thought have long been controversial in philosophy, where they become part of a larger question about the nature of human knowledge. Since many of the tacit assumptions of writers, writing teachers, and scholars in all fields rest on basic philosophical issues—What can we know? How is it that we know? What can we name?—it is useful to review briefly several key arguments made by Kant and Cassirer that are relevant to the nature of human knowledge and the relationship of language to knowledge. Cassirer deals more specifically with language than Kant does, but since Cassirer builds on Kant's transcendental critique of reason to formulate his view of symbolic forms such as myth, language, art, and science, several key points about Kant's theory provide a necessary foundation for moving from a copy theory to a symbolic view of language.

Faced with Descartes' belief that we can know nothing for certain except ourselves, and Hume's belief that causal relationships exist not in nature but in the mind and so cannot be necessary, Kant attempted to give us something to hold on to, some position that would transcend both rationalism and empiricism. Prior to Kant, copy theory in philosophy had made the object itself real, and the mind a passive recipient of that objective reality. Dissatisfied with that explanation, Kant developed his transcendental critique of reason as an alternative to copy theory. For Kant, the focal point of study is not an external object per se, but the relationship between subject and object. The interplay between our conceptual categories and the objects we perceive via sensory perception is what produces images or conceptualizations of what is "out there."

In his *Prolegomena to Any Future Metaphysics,* Kant asks: How do we know things in nature? How can a science be possible that is concerned with how we perceive and order and understand nature? He concludes that there is indeed a world existing outside of our minds; the world is not an illusion, nor is it a subjective projection of our minds. It would be "an absurdity," he says in the *Prolegomena,* "if we conceded no things in themselves or set up our experience as the only possible mode of knowing things."[35] Our subject of study when we consider nature, however, is not any thing in itself. Rather, for Kant, we are concerned with a complex of things as they become objects of possible experience for us, and also with the a priori categories according to which we construct what we know.

These categories are something we are born with. "Categories are concepts," Kant says, "which prescribe laws a priori to experiences, and therefore to nature, the sum of all appearances."[36] These categories, such as quantity, relation, quality, and modality, give us our ways of knowing. They do this a priori; that is, these concepts or categories are not based on sensory data that we obtain from the world. We simply *have* these categories which function in the construction of knowledge about the world as we experience it in space and time through our senses, or through what Kant calls our "sensuous intuitions," our images of particulars from the world.

Kant uses these categories to show that we play an active role in constructing our view of the world. We may be tempted to believe that we see nature as it really is, as a thing to be objectively perceived, measured, and known. Through the medium of poetry, this temptation to believe in a completely objective reality of the material object has been captured by Wallace Stevens, a poet inclined toward philosophical issues, in "So-and-So Reclining on Her Couch." One wants to believe that one sees the world not as artifice, but as it actually is, he suggests: "One walks easily / The unpainted shore;" one "accepts the world as anything but sculpture." Yet the woman depicted in the poem, Mrs. Pappadoupoulos, is not a detached object at all: "She floats in the contention, the flux / Between the thing as idea and / The idea as thing. / She is half who made her."[37] Although Kant might shudder at being compared to a poet, his views seem to balance similarly the contention between "thing as idea" and "idea as thing." "We are not concerned with the nature of things in themselves, which is independent of the conditions both of our sensibility and our understanding," Kant says, "but with nature as an object of possible experience" (*Prolegomena*, p. 69). In other words, we are concerned with a theoretical view of how we construct and order what we perceive in experiencing things when our innate concepts are automatically applied to nature.

Although we may never be certain about what is "out there" in nature, we have to get on with the business of living, and so we must make sense of whatever we do find. This process involves application of the pure concepts of the understanding to the content of perceptions and experience to form images. What we learn from Kant is that we are able to form judgments and eventually laws of nature not because we are merely generalizing from empirically observable facts in the material world, but because we automatically use the concepts or categories that we all possess prior to experience to construct the world as we know it. While each of us constructs reality independently, this does not mean that each of us lives in a private, idiosyncratic world. Because we share the same categories, we construct experience in essentially the same way.

Kant leads us to see that science is used not to study the actual things in the world, but to study our ways of knowing and understanding those things. The concepts of the understanding determine our view of appearances; "They [the concepts] do not derive from experiences," Kant explains, "but experience derives from them" (*Prolegomena*, p. 60). According to this view, the person is part of the experience; there is an interaction between the subject and the object that parallels conclusions of modern theoretical physics, as summarized by Jacob Bronowski: "The world is not a fixed, solid array of objects, out there, for it cannot be fully separated from our perception of it. It shifts under our gaze, it interacts with us, and the knowledge that it yields has to be interpreted by us. There is no way of exchanging information that does not demand a judgment."[38] On a similar point, Kant says: "By this judgment we know the object (though it remains unknown as it is in itself) by the universal and necessary connection of the given perceptions" (*Prolegomena*, p. 46).

Ernst Cassirer takes Kant's move away from copy theory one step further. For Cassirer, Kant's use of the word "image" suggests a view that is not quite accurate; it is still too passive. Images still seem to be given rather than made, even if Kant does say that individuals use concepts to conceptualize images from sensory data and experience. For Cassirer, images are necessary but not sufficient; from images, one goes on to construct symbols. As Charles Hendel puts it in his summary of Cassirer's view of language, "The intellect takes images and makes them serve as symbols. This is quite plain in the case of language. Words are sensuous images seen or heard but they are used with meaning and so they are employed as symbols" (*Philosophy* [1], preface, p. 50).

In stressing the importance of man's symbolizing ability, Cassirer is concerned not only with the scientific or rational thinking that had been Kant's main concern, but also with other symbolic forms such as myth, language, and art. Like all animals, Cassirer notes, man can receive and respond to stimuli. But only in man is there a symbolic system between the reception and the response, or between the receptor and effector systems. This symbolic system is what Cassirer calls the " symbolic forms," the "threads that make up this symbolic net":

No longer can man confront reality immediately; he cannot see it, as it were, face to face. Physical reality seems to recede in proportion as man's symbolic activity advances. Instead of dealing directly with the things themselves, man is in a sense constantly conversing with himself. He has so enveloped himself in linguistic forms, in artistic images, in mythical symbols or religious rites that he cannot see or know anything except by the interposition of this artificial medium. (*Essay*, p. 25)

Using this symbolic net allows us to capture and remember and emphasize parts of our perceptions and experience that would otherwise be fleeting and undifferentiated. There is more than one way of making symbols, for there are different kinds of symbolic impulses, each resulting in a unique way of conceptualizing and building upon experience. These various ways of symbolizing are represented in Cassirer's symbolic forms, each characterizing a phase in the process in which man, through human culture, seeks a "progressive self-liberation," a power to construct an increasingly ideal world (*Essay*, p. 228). We are concerned here with language as one of the symbolic forms, yet we cannot think of language as totally separate from other symbolic forms, for language retains some characteristics of what Cassirer calls mythical thinking and at the same time possesses qualities that pave the way for another symbolic form, that of scientific thinking.

For example, let us consider one aspect of the relationship between language and mythical thinking. In a culture where mythical thinking prevails, names do not merely *represent* things; rather, names *are* things. An insult to the name of a deity or person is an insult to the deity or the person per se. In a culture where linguistic rather than mythical thinking prevails as a symbolic form, logic supposedly combats and transcends the magical powers of myth. A name stands for something else; it is not synonymous with the identity of a god or a person.

Even in Western cultures that have become increasingly abstract in symbolizations—cultures in which language or scientific thinking prevail—we still find vestiges of mythical thinking with its emotive powers. My son at age four insisted on keeping photographs we took of him, and the force with which he insisted made it seem as though he thought the pictures *were* him, not a representation of him. Children chant "Sticks and stones may break my bones, but names will never hurt me," but by saying so, they seem to protest too much. Suzanne Langer, building on Cassirer's categories of language and myth, says that language with its syntax gives us logic, but at the same time, "the primacy of *names* in its [language's] make-up holds it to the hypostatic way of thinking which belongs to its twin-phenomenon, myth. Consequently, it leads us beyond the sphere of mythic and emotive thought, yet always pulls us back into it again." [39]

Language is furthermore related to scientific thinking, and is in fact necessary, according to Cassirer, for the development of the ability to form concepts in science. Cassirer claims that language is at once sensuous and intellectual, that it retains elements of myth, and that its everyday names and terms have paved the way toward scientific thinking: "It was language which taught it [the scientific concept] to survey the whole sphere of intuitive existence, which raised it from the sensuous particular to the whole, the totality of intuition" (*Philosophy* [3], p. 341). Scientific thinking is not a negation of language, but rather a continuation of it. "The road begun in language," Cassirer says, "cannot be abandoned but must be followed to its end and continued beyond this end"; the scientific concept "retains its secret bond with language. However high the pure concept may arise above the world of the senses into the realm of the ideal and intelligible, in the end it always returns in some way to that 'worldly, earthly organ' that it possesses in language" (*Philosophy* [3], pp. 329–30).

Cassirer explores language as a symbolic form in a volume of over three hundred pages, providing a comprehensive survey of historical perspectives on language as well as his own investigation of its qualities and functions. For our purposes regarding the role of language in invention, the most pertinent argument Cassirer makes is that language is a dynamic force; it is an important way by which the world is constituted. Cassirer argues repeatedly against a copy theory that makes language a passive means of reflecting what is already given. If language does copy an objective reality, Cassirer points out, then we should be able to judge one language as superior to another in making the best copy of reality (*Essay*, p. 131). But we do not judge language in this way. We do not know (as Kant shows us) what a truly objective reality is; we do not copy it with language; and we do not decide that German makes a better copy than French of a single, "true" reality.

Rather, Cassirer tells us, language leads us to construct, not merely to reproduce: "Language never merely follows the lead of impressions and perceptions, but confronts them with an independent action" (*Philosophy* [1], p. 301). Language is not, according to Cassirer, "a mere mirror, simply reflecting images or outward data"; instead, language and the other symbolic forms—myth, art, science—truly help us to see: they are "true sources of light, the prerequisite of vision" (*Philosophy* [1], p. 93). What an individual perceives and senses becomes transformed into concepts through his ability to symbolize with language. Those who would view language

as a mere copy of an objective reality, Cassirer further suggests, do
not understand that even what is commonly thought of as "copying"
is not a simple act of passive reproduction: "For this reproduction
never consists in retracing, line for line, a specific content of reality,
but in selecting a pregnant motif in that content and so producing a
characteristic 'outline' of its forms. But with this, imitation itself is
on the way to becoming *representation*, in which objects are no
longer simply received in their finished structure, but built up by
the consciousness according to their constitutive traits" (*Philosophy*
[1], p. 183). People actively choose what to name and how to name
it. Naming itself does not tell us "the truth" of a thing, but emphasizes certain aspects (*Essay*, p. 134). Even a copy, one might say, involves more than what meets the eye.

As writers, it is important for us to acknowledge that even as we
perceive/conceive and name some object or idea, we are already beginning to invent the subject matter for our discourse. Even if
thinking is not entirely linguistic, language performs a critical role
by telling us what to pay attention to. We may not want to take the
extreme position of saying that language literally creates or invents a
world in the sense of producing something completely new that isn't
there at all when language leaves the premises. Saying that a tree is
where it isn't won't make it so. But neither should we ignore the role
that language plays in how we think new thoughts. Cassirer and
others point us in what looks to be a promising direction. A symbol,
or even a sign, Cassirer stresses, helps us to perceive and analyze
and create. A chemical formula, for example, "serves not only to
represent but above all to *discover* certain logical relations. . . . It
not only offers a symbolic abbreviation for what is already known,
but opens up new roads into the unknown" (*Philosophy* [1], p. 109).
In a discussion of figures of speech used in science, S. Michael Halloran and Annette Bradford point out the heuristic function of message metaphors in genetics and of brain-as-computer metaphors in
cognitive psychology. Such metaphors are useful not only in helping
lay audiences understand science and technology, but more significantly, Halloran and Bradford claim, they help the professionals
themselves; they are metaphors "to think and work by."[40] Language
thus becomes closely associated with scientific inquiry and
discovery.

Other philosophers of language support the view that language is inventive and not merely a copy of preformulated thought. Wilhelm von Humboldt made such an argument in the early nineteenth century: "The word which is required to make the concept into a citizen of the world of thought adds to it some of its own signification," Humboldt says, "and in defining the idea, the word contains it within certain limits. . . . Because of the mutual dependency of thought and word, it is evident that languages are not really means of representing the truth that has already been ascertained, but far more, means of discovering a truth not previously known" (quoted in *Philosophy* [1], p. 159). George Steiner is a contemporary advocate of a similar idea; for him, the openness and flexibility, the ability to say what is *not* as well as what is, are what make language creative: "Every act of speech has a potential of invention, a capacity to initiate, sketch, or construct 'anti-matter.' . . . New worlds are born between the lines" (p. 228). Michael Polanyi, in *Personal Knowledge*, also describes language as a heuristic important for intellectual creation: "To learn a language or to modify its meaning is a tacit, irreversible, heuristic feat; it is a transformation of our intellectual life." For Polanyi, language is an integral part of our thinking, an anticipatory framework, and so a transformation in language affects our ways of seeing.[41]

In *Metaphors We Live By*, George Lakoff and Mark Johnson illustrate ways in which language in the form of metaphor creates rather than copies reality. They tell, for instance, of an Iranian student visiting California who had an unusual view of what the "solution of problems" meant. For him, a "solution" was not fixed or permanent or controllable; instead, "he took it to be a large volume of liquid, bubbling and smoking, containing all of your problems, either dissolved or in the form of precipitates, with catalysts constantly dissolving some problems (for the time being) and precipitating out others."[42] If we were to adopt such a metaphor, Lakoff and Johnson point out, it could truly change the ways we conceive of and act on problems. Language in metaphor, they conclude, is capable of affecting our conceptual system and creating something new.

If we do take the view that language is creative, even epistemic—if it acts as a heuristic for invention—if it shapes what we think by focusing our attention and enabling perception and cognition—if it aids understanding, and if Piaget is right in claiming that "To understand is to invent"[43]—then our research and teaching should take into account the significance of language in relation to invention in all disciplines and endeavors.

The One and the Many

The active role that language plays in constituting reality, a point so strongly argued by Cassirer, leads to another observation that is important to writers and their teachers. For Cassirer, it is not enough to say that we use language to constitute reality; it is equally important to say that we do this *together*, in a culture, and that culture, by its creations, can influence future thought. While Kant explains how we all are born with innate conceptual categories that allow us to construct reality in essentially the same way, Kant's view is primarily atomistic. He sees individuals as separate units. By looking at one person complete with categories, one could theoretically learn how all people construct a view of reality. Individuals as part of a social group or culture seem to act in parallel rather than to interact in a way that might bring about a gradual change in conceptualization. Kant does not seem to explain how something *new* can be constructed by means of human intervention, in the context of human culture: if the categories are given, are they forever fixed? How does change occur? Human beings are active in that they apply categories to the content of perception and experience, but must the categories remain constant? This is as far as Kant takes it.

Thomas Kuhn discusses this limitation of Kant's work in regard to science. Kuhn criticizes views of reality as "one real world still unknown but toward which science proceeds by successive approximation." He asks whether we should not instead be looking to a world that is a "product of a mutual accommodation between experience and language," that not only permits the existence of things-in-themselves, as Kant allows, but also conceives of categories of the mind that can change over time.[44] While Cassirer seems not to be clear about whether things-in-themselves actually exist, he does offer an answer to Kuhn's call for a way of explaining change. For Cassirer, it is not categories that change over time, but rather symbolic forms that allow culture to change over time. The categories provide a cognitive foundation from which people have fashioned symbolic forms that they use to constitute their world. By means of symbolic forms, people can change the ways in which the world is constituted.

Different symbolic forms have predominated in cultures at various times. Contemporary culture, according to Cassirer, is dominated by scientific thinking, which has in turn evolved through mythical thought and language. Generally in his works, Cassirer seems to say that the move toward scientific thought with its increasing abstractness is a definite advance that frees man's symbolic enterprise from concrete, material things and places. At other times, though, he suggests that the symbolic forms represent a variety of ways of conceptualizing experience, each of which has certain strengths and weaknesses. But the point that is important for us here is that people can act together to cause change in dominant patterns of conceptualization.

Cassirer's work on the influence that symbolic forms have on thought has been used by other linguists. According to Julius Laffal, Cassirer is a forerunner of field theorists, who stress the ways that various languages incorporate cognitive organizational patterns, chiefly through vocabulary, thus linking individual speakers to their larger culture. Each language has what the linguist Weisgerber calls its *Zwischenwelt*, an intermediate realm that contains organizing concepts developed over many years by a culture; the *Zwischenwelt* is not a copy of an external world but a way of conceptualizing it. [45] Cassirer shows us that language operates in a dialectical relationship, not only between subject and object, but also between individual and culture. He leads us to consider the ways people influence thought and language in a shared way over time, while they still maintain their status as individual language-thinkers.

It is easier to see the features of Cassirer's balanced position on language as a dialectic between individual and culture if we place his work in a context, in a spectrum of views of language as individual or social. Those taking an individual perspective stress that a person is born with a capacity for language and with cognitive structures that enable conceptualization, and that these are what chiefly account for thought and language. An individual has innate categories (Kant) or universal grammar (Chomsky) or a language potential with latent structures (Lenneberg) that unfold as he develops and expresses his inner potential. Theoretically, if one holds these views, the proper unit of study concerning language and cognition is the individual, who contains the necessary abilities and structures within.

At the opposite extreme are theorists concerned not so much with forces originating in the individual as with social forces exerted by an entity greater than and different from any individual or even a sum total of individuals. At its extreme, this view presents language and cognition as imposed by society or culture on individuals. Here we find Benjamin Whorf's view that members of speech communities are obliged to organize nature into concepts by means of linguistic systems they have tacitly agreed on, and Emile Durkheim's view that the categories that are the foundation of our conceptualizations—time, space, class, number—are of social origin, and that these categories impose themselves upon us. The importance of the social sphere is also accented by Wittgenstein, who in his later work claims that language gets its meaning from the response that comes from its use in a language community, not from the private intentions or private intelligence of an individual. Saussure, too, stresses the importance of the collectivity of language, choosing as his focus of study not the individual speaker but the general system of language, *la langue*, a tacitly accepted, collective entity not evidenced in any one individual but nevertheless exerting great influence on the communication of all members of that language system.[46]

Between these individual and social positions regarding language lies that of Cassirer and others who take what I have referred to as a dialectical position. Dialectical thinkers maintain that language and/ or cognition arise from the interplay between individuals and social or cultural phenomena. Here, with Cassirer, one finds representatives of various fields and perspectives: dialectical psychologists (Klaus Riegel); Soviet cognitive psychologists (A. R. Luria, L. S. Vygotsky); Marxist philosophers (Karl Marx, Adam Schaff); linguists with special interest in culture (Wilhelm von Humboldt, George Steiner, Ernst Cassirer); symbolic interactionist sociologists (G. H. Mead); and rhetoricians (Wayne Booth). According to a dialectical view, language, or language-thinking as Schaff calls it, is a dynamic process directed by human beings, taking place in the context of human activity. Because an individual learns language from others, her thought is to some extent connected with her social heritage; yet because she herself produces language and can make something new with it, she also makes an individual and unique contribution.

At the beginning of this chapter I ventured a guess that those who are most comfortable with scientific and technical writing would likely favor an emphasis on a view of language as social and shared, while those more inclined to the writing of poetry and fiction would prefer to view language as the expression of a private individual. Indeed, many an English department battle has arisen from this not always tacit division that is made between "functional" and "creative" prose. Such battles might best be handled by both sides declaring a victory and getting out, and on the way, looking for a philosophy that will accommodate and indeed exploit the potential of language to be at the same time private and public, individual and social. The dialectical view I have been describing is an attempt to articulate this intermediary position.

When we consider language with its private and public dimensions as a source of invention, we inevitably find ourselves talking about a dialectic of individuals (or groups) with both societies and cultures. Do we mean to say that language is social, or cultural, or both? Different theorists have interpreted these terms variously, and this cannot be the place for an extensive discussion of their definitions. In *The Inquiring Mind*, George Boas, who emphasizes the close connection between language and social groups, prefers to use the words "interpersonal" or "social" rather than "cultural," and explains why. No one invents in his own language, Boas says; language is absorbed from others. "If I speak of this as interpersonal or social rather than as cultural," he goes on, "it is because I wish to preserve the possibility of society's being composed of social groups which have little homogeneity as a collection. I wish also to preserve the possibility of a single individual's belonging to several social groups in which not merely his speech but also his system of values will change."[47]

Cassirer, on the other hand, prefers to talk of language and the other symbolic forms as links between individuals and culture rather than individuals and social groups. Perhaps he is more interested in the very broad sweep or collective that Boas wishes to avoid. It seems that for Cassirer, man is more than merely social, or is social in a special sense in that he creates new ways of conceptualizing reality by means of symbolic forms. Cassirer agrees with

Aristotle that man is social, and he also agrees with Plato that one ought not study man in his individual life, as Socrates did, but in his political and social life as well: the story of man in terms of personal experience is recorded, Cassirer says, in small characters that are illegible, whereas "the nature of man is written in capital letters in the nature of the state" (*Essay*, p. 63). Still, Cassirer claims, a view of man as social and political is not comprehensive enough to capture the distinctive abilities that man has. Other animals, after all, exhibit social behavior and organization as well. And long before man organized the political state, he had tried other ways to organize thoughts and feelings with symbolic forms. What Cassirer calls the "definition of man in terms of human culture" involves the symbolic forms. Culture, for him, seems to involve this "higher form of society" that includes language, art, myth, religion, and science.

Culture involves the creative acts of which man is capable with these symbolic forms: "Man cannot find himself, he cannot become aware of his individuality, save through the medium of social life. . . . Man, like the animals, submits to the rules of society but, in addition, he has an active share in bringing about, and an active power to change, the forms of social life" (*Essay*, p. 223). Human culture seems more abstract and more encompassing than the social realm; it is perhaps society to the *n*th power, involving the creative power of social groups. Culture, according to Cassirer, seems consistent at least in part with Sapir's definition of culture as what society thinks and does. As one of the symbolic forms, then, language is integrally woven into culture as one important way by which society makes something from itself to live on after it is gone.

Even when the inventor is alone, invention has its social elements, not the least of which is language. In summary, here is a sequence of five related assertions pertaining to the role of language in a social perspective on rhetorical invention:

1. *Thought and language are intimately related*—so much so, in fact, that they may be referred to a a "thought/language" unit. They are not identical, but it is appropriate to consider them as integrally connected in a dynamic process. Vygotsky's "knot" metaphor represents the linking of verbal thought and language in the individual who has passed infancy. For Vygotsky, the thought/word relationship is "not a thing but a process, a continual movement back and

forth from thought to word and from word to thought. . . . Thought is not merely expressed in words; it comes into existence through them"; "A thought," Vygotsky says, "may be compared to a cloud shedding a shower of words" (pp. 125, 150). Language is thus not merely a copy of thoughts that are essentially extralinguistic or pre-linguistic; rather, language is integrally related to thought.

2. *Thought/language is active and constitutive.* It is not a passive copy of an objective external reality, but rather, it is an active agent in a process of constituting reality.

3. *Thought/language is social.* It is not only individual or private, but occurs as a dialectic between individual and social spheres. "Human thought is consummately social," Clifford Geertz has said: "social in its origins, social in its function, social in its forms, social in its applications."[48] Furthermore, all language, whether it is used in a poem or a technical report, operates flexibly as part of a continuum that includes both private and public dimensions.

4. *Rhetorical invention occurs to a great extent through thought/ language.* While invention may occur in nonlinguistic modes of thinking (through visual images, for example), in contemporary culture—and especially, perhaps, in Western culture—language/thinking is a primary mode of cognition, and a primary source of invention as well.

5. *Rhetorical invention is active and social.* Since rhetorical invention occurs largely through thought/language, its features are similar to those of thought/language. Thus, rhetorical invention, like thought/language, is both active and social. If one holds that language is exclusively a copy of an existing reality (e.g., external objects or internal thoughts), then it is a mirror only, and thus would seem not to figure in invention except as a way of reporting what has already been perceived or thought. But if one holds, as I do, the view that language is active in constituting reality, then language indeed deserves to be considered as an active partner in the invention process, whether invention be thought of in a rhetorical or a generic sense.

Invention is *active* in the sense that according to contemporary definitions, invention is increasingly regarded as the act of creating something, not only as the act of retrieving and rendering what was previously known. And invention is *social* in that even while it occurs in an individual, it is heavily influenced by that individual's relationship to others through the social entity of language as well as through social structures, forms, purposes, and practices.

In this chapter I have suggested that reality is constituted through a dialectic between subject and object that occurs by way of language, and that we think of this process of constituting the world through language as something we do both together and alone, socially as well as individually. Language plays an active role in the generation of what we come to know and say, and in that role, it demonstrates the inextricable involvement of social elements in invention.

6

Implications of
a Social Perspective on
Rhetorical Invention

FROM THE NINETEENTH CENTURY TO THE PRESENT, RHETORICAL invention in composition has been rooted in radical individualism. I have argued that a view of invention as the act of an atomistic individual producing a discrete text is severely limited—that it misleadingly divorces the individual from the social realm and fails to account for much of what happens when writers invent. Invention should be reconceived, I have suggested, as a social act: one in which individuals interact with society and culture in a distinctive way to create something. With this view, invention may be seen as an act encompassing symbol-using activities such as speaking and writing, often involving more than one person, and extending over time through a series of social transactions and texts. The generation of what one comes to know and say is brought to completion by others who receive and execute the action.

What implications does this view have for writing, for scholarship and research, and for the teaching of writing? Changes compatible with a social view of invention have in fact already begun. In recent years there has been growing advocacy for teaching composition as a collaborative learning process of writers with teachers, writers with peer tutors, and writers with readers in workshop groups. Articles, books, workshops, and conference papers have suggested ways to structure and improve these various interactions.[1] At the same time, the increasing attention being paid to writing across the curriculum and writing in the world of work reminds us of the importance of composition directed towards something other than the theme for English 101. Since much of the inventing done in other disciplines and professions is collaborative, these developments encourage us to regard invention as a social enterprise.

New directions are evident not only in teaching but also in research. The development of naturalistic research on writers in their normal composing situations makes it possible to study invention in a more realistic and comprehensive way than, say, by looking at one writer in an experimental setting who invents material to produce one draft of a text.[2] When we observe inventors over a period of time in their natural habitats, we find that in fact they *do* interact with others, although such activities have often been "controlled out" in experimental studies. In all these endeavors—collaborative instruction, writing across the curriculum, and naturalistic research—changes in practice have preceded the articulation of corresponding theory. Clarifying our theoretical perspective should enable us to see more clearly what has already been accomplished and hasten the process of change already under way.

Beyond these incipient changes in teaching and research, a view of invention as a social act has many additional implications. My discussion of these is meant to be suggestive rather than exhaustive. At present it is probably impossible to see fully what this perspective implies; like many composition theories and pedagogies, this book does not completely escape the individualism that has infused all arenas—political, economic, intellectual, and social—for so long that it is difficult to avoid entirely its impress. Gregory Bateson remarks that "we are most of us governed by epistemologies that we know to be wrong."[3] Given the status quo, however, there are a number of things we can begin to do as writers, researchers, and teachers to put into practice a view of invention as a social act.

Implications for Writers

As writers who adopt this perspective, we will regard invention as an act that involves both the creation and the continuing use of a text, extending through readers' responses, revision, publication, criticism, and defense. We will value invention not just as a method of retrieving what we already know, but as a process that constitutes our inquiry. We will understand the value of cultivating relationships with those with whom we invent and of attending more carefully to ways of enabling the creativity of others. It is in our interest to recognize the influence of social collectives on what and how we invent, attempting to make explicit their tacit rules so we can decide which to abide by or what the consequences may be if we do not.

Writers in all discourse communities should attempt to clarify and possibly expand the prevailing sense of what constitutes collaboration and how it should be acknowledged. Many of us are careful to acknowledge what we borrow from texts by dead or absent authors, but less than thorough in noting contributions from living people with whom we speak and think and work. Attempting to give proper credit prompts us to ask ourselves questions that are not easy to answer. Did I get that idea from a conversation with X? Or is it an idea I had thought of earlier, which X helped to develop or confirm? If Y and Z help me revise a manuscript, how should I acknowledge them? Or needn't I? If I thank them in a footnote, will someone think I'm dropping names? Will they be implicated if my book gets negative reviews? Before I acknowledge them, should I ask if they object? If a book evolves from a series of talks Z and I have over lunch, who is the inventor? Who should own the copyright? Is it ethical for me merely to dedicate it "to Z, without whom . . ."?

Not everyone who assists invention must be part-author, but there may well be better ways than we have at present to document the various contributions. For instance, a 1970 survey of psychologists by Donald Spiegel and Patricia Keith-Spiegel found that more than one-quarter of the respondents supported a proposal requiring each psychology journal article to include a footnote detailing the contributions of authors and nonauthors alike, taking note of such tasks as research design, data collection and analysis, technical assistance, and manuscript preparation.[4] "Think what it would mean," Dale Spender has said, "if we began to devise a referencing system that catered to collective ideas?"[5] The complicated question of how to assign credit for a collaborative invention is inextricably tied to a larger question about what "counts" as a significant intellectual contribution to one's community and one's field. Widely espoused ideals of collegiality and interdisciplinary research are in fact constantly undermined by individualistic assumptions built into the structure of academia in general and the English department in particular. The typical English department faculty member is supposed to be a one-person show who must be able to teach-write-serve-research alone, compete for limited resources, and manage all the while to appear cooperative. Rarely are individuals evaluated on the basis of how well they interact with others to invent or how much they contribute to the inventions of others.

While collaboration is more common in some areas of science, medicine, and engineering, English professors are uneasy about dealing with the issues collaborative invention raises. How, for example, should a department evaluate (hire, fire, tenure, and promote) someone who has coauthored a number of publications? Is collaboration a positive sign showing the ability to cooperate and maximize the strengths of individuals, or does it imply that an individual *must* collaborate to compensate for inherent weaknesses? If an individual is noted in a colleague's book as having significantly influenced the development of the author's ideas, should that be noted with passing interest or counted as a major contribution? If a writer takes care to acknowledge explicitly the assistance of others, does it mean that she is trying to be free of the need to declare proprietary ownership of ideas, or does it mean that she depends too much on others?

Underlying such questions is a persisting suspicion that if a person were *really* inventive, she would be entirely self-sufficient. The prevailing view of the atomistic inventor makes it difficult to develop new ways of understanding, acknowledging, and judging a wide range of collaborative efforts. It seems likely that teachers in the humanities, knowing consciously or unconsciously that collaboration is suspect, either avoid it or downplay its effects on their efforts as individuals. If we who make up academic communities are not yet confident of our ability to evaluate, promote, and fund collaborative efforts, we should at least begin to re-examine longstanding attitudes and practices. Spared the Columbus complex—the myth of the atomistic discoverer—we can try to create communities that foster invention. There will always be great need for individual initiative, but no matter how inventive an individual wants to be, he will be influenced for better or for worse by the intellectual company he keeps. On top of Mt. Mansfield in Vermont, there are thirty-year-old trees that are only three feet tall. If a tree begins to grow taller, extending beyond the protection of the others, it dies. The moral for inventors: Plant yourself in a tall forest if you hope to have ideas of stature.

Implications for Researchers and Scholars

Research on rhetorical invention has tended to focus on the atomistic inventor composing a single text. Thus it is not surprising that we haven't noticed the social aspects of invention; we have in fact arranged the research situation to exclude social interaction, thus eliminating what are often significant elements in invention. As researchers and scholars, adopting a social perspective on invention leads us to broaden the scope of our inquiry to take into account the social realm and treat cognition as a social as well as an individual phenomenon. Researchers will examine the relationship of a text to other texts and to conversations that precede and follow it; they will also take note of the writer's relationships to other people—internalized censors, actual editors, collaborators—who affect invention. We may continue to study the testimony of writers to follow their processes of inquiry, including their conversations, research activities, and other actions. We should also examine acknowledgment practices in academic and nonacademic contexts to see how the contributions of others have been perceived and documented, thus building a foundation on which to base possible change.[6] Literary scholars can elect to reinterpret literary biography, concentrating less on the psychology of the individual writer's mind and turning to what Edward Mendelson describes as "external and social matters ranging from the economics of publications to the larger questions of a modern writer's social role."[7] Composition researchers may use the converging approaches evident in naturalistic studies, including interviews, self-reports of internal dialogues, and observations of a larger social collective with rules, conventions, and expectations. In all these instances, we study a larger locus of inventive activity, a social matrix rather than an isolated writer and text.

If we extend to rhetorical invention Michel Foucault's view of discourse as an endless potentiality that is occasionally evidenced in speech or writing, then we will study invention as a process extending over time, a process both enabled and manifested through talk and texts. We will conduct longitudinal studies, tracking invention as it occurs over months or years. Such research might involve writing done on the job or writing done across the curriculum, in more than one course. To draw a parallel with Fernand Braudel's historical concepts, we would concern ourselves with the *longue durée* rather than *l'histoire événementielle*—that is, with the longer time span as opposed to the brief episode. This shift would help to correct an overemphasis on the isolated individual who appears to make a discovery at a clearly identifiable time. Criticizing this tendency, Thomas Kuhn observes that "we need a new vocabulary and concepts for analyzing events like the discovery of oxygen." To state simply that "oxygen was discovered" by one individual at a given point in time obscures a complex discovery process that occurred between 1774 and 1777, involved at least Priestley and Lavoisier (and perhaps C. W. Scheele), and required not only the observation that a certain gas existed but also a conceptualization of what it was.[8] It is important that we frame our studies of invention in any field to call into question (or at least avoid taking for granted) the concept of the autonomous inventor wrested from an evolving process in a community.

In composition, theories of invention should be reconsidered to see how they support or contest a view of invention as a social act. Scholars may want to re-evaluate theories (and textbooks derived from them) that are primarily Platonic in their focus on writing as an individual's self-expression, supplementing them with inventional theories that take into account the social aspects of invention—for instance, the nature of collaboration and the role of collectives. Through research we can clarify the ways in which writers collaborate to invent in various contexts, in and out of the classroom. To contribute to the international need for peaceful resolution of conflicts, we must study and develop ways of inventing collaboratively in the especially constrained circumstances of negotiations. As we plan case studies of negotiating sessions that extend over time, we should become familiar with the literature concerning negotiation and conflict resolution, a fairly young field of specialization from which we can learn even as we contribute a rhetorical perspective.

We must reinterpret the history of invention. Borrowing from Harold Lasswell's concept of an "ecology of innovation,"[9] we should study the ecology of invention—the ways ideas arise and are nurtured or hindered by interaction with social context and culture. To do this, we will observe groups that have produced new ideas or inventions to see what it is about the group or the dynamics of individuals interacting within it that fosters invention. We will also do historical studies of invention (including social history, social biography, collective biography) in which we examine the social relationships of writers with other thinkers, or those of inventors with collaborators who aid invention in a variety of ways. We can study and teach about invention as it occurs in temporary communities that emerge spontaneously (e.g., the avant-garde writers clustering at Sylvia Beach's Shakespeare and Company bookshop or Frances Steloff's Gotham Book Mart) or in communities brought together to solve problems (scientists developing nuclear weapons in the Manhattan Project).

While we will continue to study the individual inventor, we will look at one's processes and contexts of invention through the lens of a social perspective. This means that the interactions of an individual with others in social contexts will serve as one important focal point for study. For instance, Stephen Jay Gould builds on the historical research of Frank Sulloway to reassess the legend of how Charles Darwin, "alone at sea, transform[ed] the intellectual world in splendid mental isolation."[10] Gould argues that contrary to what is commonly believed, Darwin developed his theory of evolution during the year *after* his famed voyage to the Galápagos Islands on the *Beagle*, and that Darwin's work depended on his interactions with others in England: with shipmates whose collections of specimens from the voyage differed from his in important ways, and with experts—paleontologist Richard Owen and ornithologist John Gould—who analyzed his specimens and corrected errors. Without minimizing Darwin's ability to synthesize facts and formulate a new explanation—his genius for seeing with "an enlarged vision"—Stephen Jay Gould stresses the fact that Darwin did not accomplish this alone: "Scientific achievement is also a communal activity, not a hermit's achievement. Where would Darwin have been in 1837 without Gould, Owen, and the active scientific life of London and Cambridge?"[11]

Turning to anthropology for another example, consider the explicitly ecological terms with which Mary Catherine Bateson describes how her mother, Margaret Mead, generated and dispersed new ideas "when she acted in living systems."[12] Bateson tells of a ship design created by ecologist John Todd to be named for Mead, one that represents Mead's way of propagating new ideas: it would be a "wind-driven ecological hope ship" moving about the world, "pick-ing up seeds and seedlings of rare plants . . . and growing them at sea so that they can be ready to plant or introduce as new crops on arrival in the next port" (M. C. Bateson, p. 191).

Apparently Mead did not simply transport ideas that would spring up of their own accord. Bateson observes, "She was a one-person conference," who traveled through many conversations and used a notebook as a catalyst:

> The notebook stands in my mind for a whole way of working whereby she was constantly taking in new material and using it, incorporating reac-tions, so that an interesting piece of work she heard about in Florida would be talked about in Topeka and synthesized with what someone was thinking or writing in Boston, elaborated in Cincinnati, incorporated in a lecture in California. She tried to be conscientious about giving credit and would often put people working on related matters in touch with each other, but no amount of care for references to formal pieces of work could sufficiently reflect the extent to which all her speeches and writing represented a legion of voices. (M. C. Bateson, p. 191)

In fact, Bateson claims, Mead's notebook itself became a tool that invited others' participation: "consciously or unconsciously, we used to try to say things that would stimulate her to get it out and write them down, and then one would have the feeling of having contrib-uted a piece to the complex jigsaw puzzle she was putting to-gether. . . . Five years later we would be talking of the same topic, and she would say, 'That was your point, you know. That was a piece you gave me'" (M. C. Bateson, p. 192). Mead's way of interacting with people and ideas by writing and speaking, affecting and being affected by such transactions, serves as a case in point to indicate that invention may be studied from a social perspective even when its agent is an individual.

Implications for Teachers

Practical Implications
A view of invention as a social act has significant practical implica-tions for the teaching of writing, some of which I will outline before

turning to its broader implications for understanding the nature of knowledge and the structure of the curriculum.

Co- and group-authorship. A major implication of this perspective for teaching is a new emphasis on a variety of inventive "units" such as the dyad, triad, or group. As teachers, we need not automatically assume that we will assign tasks to individuals who go off by themselves to invent, nor should we necessarily assign only to individuals the praise, blame, or grade for what is invented. In many work situations in which our students will write (or are already writing), invention will necessarily involve some types of collaboration. When our students include those who will be technical writers on a corporate product development team, or future journalists who will rely heavily on interviews, or scientist/writers doing team research—to name but a few examples—we should guide them through social interchanges such as interviews and collaborative invention and critique sessions. These are an integral part of the writing process, and thus they should be legitimized and practiced in the writing class.

Teaching invention from a social perspective means teaching students how to go about solving the problems that inevitably arise in collaborative invention. We can make assignments in ways that explicitly invite students to think through ideas in the company of others and to carry out interviews with people who are important sources of information and opinion. We can send students out of the classroom to public meetings, fraternity meetings, or legislative sessions, where they can observe the many ways of enabling and hindering creative ideas. In the classroom we can use role-playing and case studies to teach ways of generating ideas in constrained circumstances that require negotiation. Learning to invent in communities will do more than enable success in classrooms or careers. It is absolutely essential to achieving peace and, indeed, maintaining life on this planet in the twentieth century and beyond. To enable students to use invention in this broad sense, as a truly social act, we must become alert to opportunities for students to write to effect social change at any level, helping them to find what Richard Ohmann has called "a middle ground . . . between passing English 101 and saving mankind: the students' uses of their literacy for social or personal ends in society."[13] Invention can be taught not as an exercise one must do to produce a paper for a course, but as an indispensible part of solving a problem or addressing a concern.

To convey this concept in the composition course, a teacher can help students identify issues in need of attention, issues that would involve writing and speaking as appropriate modes of action. A class can subdivide into groups, each concentrating on tasks related to one central purpose, thus dividing the labor but working toward a common goal. An alternative is to divide the class into groups, each of which defines its own issue, in which case the issues may or may not relate to each other. While this approach offers variety and allows for collaborative learning, it does not contribute as effectively to developing a sense of identity and community in the class as a whole. Still another alternative is to ask the class to frame a central issue in terms of a pro and con argument, dividing into teams to defend each point of view. The defense (involving collaborative work in small groups subdivided from each team) may involve interviews, library research, written arguments, oral presentations, and possibly a culminating debate to which guests are invited from the campus and the larger community. This arrangement adds the interest of friendly competition, but all in the service of exploring and proposing solutions to one central problem.

Choosing the issue to study in such courses is an important matter in which students should play a major role. One clearly appropriate area for a composition course (though certainly not the only one) would be the study of language in various communities, with students acting as ethnographic researchers. The goal, as James A. Reither has put it, would be to "immerse" students in discourse communities through a workshop approach in which "students and teacher function but as co-investigators, with reading and writing being used collaboratively to conduct the inquiry."[14]

Suppose, for instance, that a university's English department is considering developing a minor in writing, and that students in a composition course choose that as an issue needing attention. They divide into groups according to their major fields and then study the special problems and needs faced by writers (in school and on the job) in computer science, engineering, and management. They observe the writing practices of students, professors, and professionals employed in industry. They interview writers and readers; observe writers who collaborate to write; and analyze textbooks, memoranda, letters, articles, and reports. Taking into consideration what they discover about the major characteristics of writing in their fields and about the typical problems that writers encounter, the student ethnographers draw conclusions about how a minor in writing should be designed to suit students' needs. They choose the most appropriate ways to synthesize and present their conclusions: writing a report to a department chair or dean; meeting with a faculty curriculum committee; organizing a class presentation to which other students and concerned faculty are invited; or publishing articles in the campus newspaper. Perhaps they submit their work to a journal for composition teachers, who stand to benefit from the students' familiarity with fields that English teachers can never hope to know in such particularity.

While we as teachers develop these and other classroom activities, we should at the same time re-evaluate traditional educational practices based on individualistic values. Consider but two examples: the traditional view of independent dissertation research and the time-honored practice of assigning academic work and grades to individuals. The commonly accepted purpose of a dissertation is to show that one can do "independent, original research." Granted that we value new, worthwhile ideas, to what extent is it admirable or realistic to think of this as totally "independent"? Does "independent" mean one must act alone? Many an A.B.D. who has negotiated a thesis through numerous sessions with committee members would hardly qualify in that regard. Perhaps it is more profitable to think of such a project as a demonstration of one's ability to *integrate* or *synthesize* social heritage and social influence (not to mention the ideas of dissertation committee members) to make something new, thus exhibiting what Richard Ohmann describes as an important characteristic of the inventive person: "Out of whatever he is given he makes more. He stands in an active relationship to circumstances and events."[15]

In addition to the typical view of the dissertation process, another practice permeated with individualistic assumptions is that of assigning both work and grades to individuals rather than groups. When teachers begin to design collaborative learning experiences, they often take care to provide an "escape clause" allowing any student the option to work on an individual project rather than to be part of the group. This practice, however, has implications that run counter to the entire philosophy of collaboration. It suggests that individuals need not find a function in their social group and that groups need not deal with (or be responsible for) individuals. Permitting individuals to escape from their roles in the group allows all parties to abdicate responsibilities even as it deprives them of the opportunity to learn how to negotiate their desires and needs while solving a mutual problem. Educator Ewa Pytowska has noted that while most American teachers believe that fostering a cohesive classroom community is but one possible teaching strategy among many, she believes it is the *only* strategy, "or better, the only philosophy and the only attitude which helps one's students become individualistic in the true sense of the word 'individuality' . . . that which sprouts in each person who is tied to others by the rope of a common goal and the limits of a common path." [16]

When students work in groups toward a common goal, how are teachers to evaluate them? No longer do we carry home a stack of essays authored by individuals, each of which receives a separate grade. The evaluation should take into account a student's ability to interact constructively with others in the various roles of reader, critic, and collaborator. Moreover, students should share in the evaluation of the group's work, as should those outside the class who represent an audience in a position to be affected by the group's information and arguments—for instance, local politicians or university administrators invited to a class presentation or debate. [17] Discussing various ways to teach writing in groups, Richard M. Coe argues in favor of grading the work of the group as a whole, with each student ultimately responsible not simply for a section (in which case, each might do just that section), but for the entire project. "To some extent this violates our standard sense of 'fairness,'" Coe notes, "but that is because our culture does not encourage collective responsibility. In the real world, collectively produced writing is judged according to how well the writing-as-a-whole accomplishes its purpose, so collective grading is realistic." [18] While teachers will no doubt continue to make some assignments to be completed by individuals who receive an individual grade, it seems entirely appropriate to grade collectively the work that is produced, for the most part, by collaboration, thus fostering a classroom climate in which it is in a student's interest to cooperate rather than compete.

Single Authorship. Taking a social perspective on invention does not mean, of course, that one must think only of inventing and writing in pairs or groups. Central to this perspective, as we have previously seen, is the point that invention is appropriately viewed as social in nature even when the primary inventor is an individual. To teach about invention, then, there are attitudes and practices we should convey about situations in which individuals are the primary authors of texts. We can suggest how and when writers may involve internal "others" (through inner dialogues with imagined readers or with a critical inner self). Frank D'Angelo, for instance, encourages students to write dialogues to prepare for argumentation and persuasion.[19] Furthermore, teachers can adapt and develop heuristics that encourage a writer to examine social elements and social relationships as a way of inventing. The particle-wave-field system of tagmemic invention can be used to look at a literary author as an individual, then as an individual whose experiences and subjects vary over time, and finally (and perhaps most importantly for our purposes) as a writer-among-others and a participant in society and culture.[20] To increase students' awareness that invention has its social aspects even when the written product has a single author, we can show them models of written acknowledgments and ask them to write their own acknowledgments for essays they compose, as Elaine Maimon and her coauthors from Beaver College have suggested.[21] Or students might write prefatory notes telling how and why their essays were written and who assisted them at various points, as Donald Graves has done with each chapter in his collection of articles, *A Researcher Learns to Write.*[22]

Inventors in Social Contexts. While we as teachers of composition will work with individual writers as well as writers in pairs and groups, in all of these circumstances we must take into account writers' inextricable connections to social realms beyond the classroom. Since neither the individual nor the group invents in a vacuum, we must consider the relationships of inventors to other social groups and institutions, all of which impose on inventors various rules, preferences, conventions, and restrictions.

In recent years, the increase in older adults returning to college campuses has no doubt helped to make us less naive about invention. These students' work experiences give rise to writing problems that cannot be solved by suggestions that they need only express what is hidden deep within, or that they are free to include in their writing any ideas or information they may have. It would be naive to expect a student who writes for a hospital newsletter to add details about, say, the problems of the hospital's current system of storing x-rays, when her article must be approved by a public relations director who does not want the existing system to appear too inefficient even though it is about to be replaced. Or consider the case of an engineering student who tells a writing tutor that his advisor will not allow him to draw certain conclusions in his thesis because the agency sponsoring the research would discover that the work was essentially completed and would cut off funding. It would be beside the point for the tutor to suggest that this student try free-writing or tagmemics to come up with new material for his conclusion. A writing teacher who critiques a technical writer's article about innovations in computer documentation may sense that specific details or quotations from company authorities would improve it. But if the company employing the writer must approve the article before she can publish it, and if their policy is never to reveal specifics, she will not solve this problem by looking within and inventing as she pleases. Diplomacy is the rudder of invention.

Given such situations, what is a writing teacher or tutor to do? That is difficult to say. We can help writers to articulate their concerns and their perceptions of the constraints they face. We can talk about ways they might test the accuracy of their perceptions, or work around their constraints, or discuss problems with those responsible for creating and enforcing certain rules and policies. The writers and their supervisors may or may not try to change the status quo. What we cannot do is act as if these problems do not exist, as if people's jobs are not at stake, as if invention means asking the journalist's five W's and an H without taking into account the very real implications that these choices have for writers in their social contexts.

The Nature of Knowledge and the Structure of the Curriculum

Up to this point, I have outlined a number of practical implications of a social perspective for the teaching of writing. Perhaps more importantly, this perspective helps to reveal problems inherent in received views of the nature of knowledge, questionable views which in turn affect dramatically the structure and aims of the postsecondary curriculum. These views are as follows:

- Knowledge is represented in language rather than constituted by it;
- "Hard" knowledge is mechanistically gained by the accumulation of objective facts and is "discovered" by an atomistic individual;
- Knowledge in the university is best studied and taught by division into separate disciplines and discrete courses.

Each of these lingering assumptions is called into question by a social perspective on invention. The first assumption, discussed at length in the previous chapter, is the view that language is, at best, the garb that finished thought puts on and at worst, an obstacle to pure thought. By contrast, a social perspective on invention stresses the importance of language: as a socially created and shared symbol system with which we (by and large) invent, both individually and collaboratively; and as that which constitutes knowledge. We should teach student writers what is at stake in the debate about the complex relationships of language, thought, and reality. Textbooks and theoretical works in many disciplines should be rewritten to address more carefully the complex issues concerning language. Much that is misunderstood about language, especially in postsecondary education, has come about not only because the *wrong* things have been said or written, but because in many cases, *nothing* has been said or written. While our entire curriculum is based on language, its role seems to be taken for granted in advanced years of education. Kenneth Bruffee, in calling for changes in liberal education to correspond to changing conceptions of the structure of knowledge, stresses the importance of language as "the supreme means by which communities have created and continue to create knowledge by negotiating consensus and assent." Language, Bruffee concludes, should be the foundation of a restructured postsecondary education that highlights the processes of communication and of collaborative work and thinking.[23]

Such an emphasis on language can be dealt with in part in writing courses, but should by no means be restricted to them, nor restricted to academia. We should seek, for example, to persuade those who write about science and technology—and their employers—that writing and language are closely connected with invention or innovation, that they do much more than merely transmit work that has already been completed. We can encourage employers to recognize and support this view of language by acknowledging its

value for all workers and by giving proper recognition and re-
muneration to writers who are involved in active, creative work—as
happens more frequently in the computer industry, where it is increasingly apparent that documentation is a product inseparable
from the computer.

In addition to pointing toward an expanded conception of the role
of language in creating knowledge, a social perspective on invention
helps dissuade us of another assumption about knowledge that lin-
gers despite harsh attacks in recent years. This assumption, briefly
put, is that "hard" knowledge in mathematics and the sciences is arrived at by mechanistic accumulation of facts objectively verified by
testing in relation to fixed laws and previously established facts. The
twentieth century has challenged this view, arguing instead (via
Einstein and Heisenberg, among others) that what is known is a
matter of probability rather than certainty, influenced by the ob-
server's frame of reference and instruments and symbol systems. On
the subject of scientific knowledge, as we have seen, Thomas Kuhn
is among those who argue that knowledge is constructed by means
of ongoing argument, and eventually, acceptance by a consensus of a
community of thinkers. In delineating this changing view of knowledge, Kenneth Bruffee states that its implication for education is
that we as humanists ought to study and teach the communitarian
nature of knowledge, and that we can do so if, instead of concentrating solely on great individuals, we "stress instead their role in helping to create a consensus among the members of their own society
and culture, among their artistic and intellectual peers."[24] A social
view of invention, with its emphasis on the constant dialectic of individuals with others and with the socioculture, offers a theoretical
foundation for attempts to study and to teach the communitarian nature of knowledge. It also lends support for a variety of pedagogical
changes, from expanding opportunities for collaborative learning, to
allowing the grading of groups as well as individuals, to restructur-
ing the physical environment to reduce the number of classrooms
designed for large lectures while increasing flexible work spaces
where students and teachers can work conveniently in pairs and
groups.

Finally, an understanding of invention as a social act helps direct
us toward a possible synthesis of the fragmentation of knowledge
existing in the academic disciplines. Not only has academia isolated

the inventor, but it has segmented invention, declaring certain kinds of knowledge and certain ways of knowing as the province of distinct disciplines, departments, majors, and courses. Despite universal calls for interdisciplinary efforts, such aims are difficult to achieve because they run counter to the specialization ingrained in contemporary institutions.

There is fortunately still some debate about whether or not there remains any disciplinary territory for composition theorists and teachers to claim. There may be good reasons for us to concern ourselves less with defining our separate territory and more with expanding our role as interdisciplinary agents. Writing across the curriculum—or, for our purposes here, inventing across the curriculum, using writing as a mode of inquiry—is potentially a radical movement which, given more time and a more fully developed theoretical base, could do much to revolutionize the structuring of knowledge in the university curriculum. This movement points toward alternative ways to teach writing and inquiring in all disciplines and a departure from the practice of localizing writing instruction in the freshman composition course, where invention has too often been presented as if it occurs in a social and intellectual vacuum, motivated primarily by the student's need to fill pages to pass a course.

Integrating writing with learning in the entire curriculum leads the way to truly interdisciplinary efforts. It may influence the organization of such things as credits and courses. Perhaps, for one thing, the usefulness of the "course" as we know it should be questioned. One alternative or supplement to the writing course, for example, could be to work with a developing portfolio of a student's writing over several years, in a manner reminiscent of the seventeenth century tutorial system at Harvard. Students could meet individually and in small groups with a rhetorician/advisor for ongoing conversations evolving around a series of texts: notes about classes and conversations, an idea journal, course papers from all disciplines, drafts of work in progress. Since true innovation is often the outgrowth of a series of smaller, sometimes imperceptible steps, broadening our view of invention to include a range of inventive efforts over time and across disciplines should help us and our students to nurture and to track invention.

Another writing across the curriculum possibility (related to "cap-

stone" courses taken by upper level students at some institutions)
would be to ask juniors or seniors to identify an issue or research
problem of interest that has not been adequately addressed. An individual or a small group of students could propose the issue and
meet with a writing advisor and an advisor from another appropriate
discipline. With this arrangement, invention begins, in the classical
sense, with identification of a "stasis," which John Gage has described as "the point of disagreement between a writer or speaker
and an audience." Composition courses usually lack this concept of
stasis, Gage explains, in that they compel people to write whether
or not they have any need to address a problem; it is possible, however, to reintroduce the concept of stasis by helping students to
identify rhetorical situations, areas about which they already know a
good deal, and on which they have opinions that may differ from
those of others, thus leading to the possibility of true argument.[25]

Experiences such as these—the long-range tutorial and the "cap-
stone" rhetorical situation—are admittedly difficult to implement,
expecially where there are large numbers of students and a faculty
under pressure to publish rather than to teach. However, even
these sketchy descriptions should serve to illustrate the kinds of
educational options that could help at least some students to use
writing as a mode of inquiry in a collaborative way that enables and
even encourages them (and their teachers) to integrate knowledge
across disciplinary boundaries. In keeping with a social view of invention, such educational experiences create social contexts in
which students and professors collaborate over a period of time,
through a series of transactions and texts, to work toward a solution
and, ideally, to create something original. Writing across the curriculum thus may not only improve students' writing in all disciplines (itself a laudable goal), but also challenge conventional ways
of compartmentalizing knowledge in the curriculum.

Conclusion

If we question the radical individualism that pervades our culture
as well as our composition theories, then our understanding of invention will differ from what has recently prevailed. We will view
the "self" that invents, as Wayne Booth suggests, as "a kind of

value-permeated field in which a value-permeated universe creates
and is in turn 'processed' by what is really a history of selves in interaction with selves."[26] Decisions about what ideas to accept or reject,
and what to include in discourse—what constitutes a "good reason"—will be recognized as based not on private wisdom alone but
on social consensus. Whether what appear to be good reasons really
are good reasons, Booth says, "can only be determined in social or
potentially social converse with reasonable men, not in private, isolated, 'logical,' consultation of my atomic self and its wisdom."[27] The
inventing self is thus socially constituted, and what is invented is
judged according to its social contexts. Throughout this study I have
explored many variations on the theme that the individual and social realms are co-existing and mutually defining, with their dialectic necessarily impinging on invention.

The history of invention, in both its rhetorical and generic uses,
is writ large in terms of the atomistic I. In many cases, no doubt, we
should be acknowledging the individual's inventive efforts. The individual has a particular way of interacting with what she inherits socially and culturally, and she is capable of offering something unique
in that regard. I do not wish to slight in any way the work or ideas or
actions initiated by individuals, nor to suggest that individuals abdicate responsibility for their ideas and actions.

What I have tried to do is to look at the individual through a
wider lens to see the inventor's relationships with a social heritage of
ideas and with other people both living and dead, in a process occurring through socially shared language and culture. I began this
study with Martin Buber's description of the other that is always
present in the internal conversations constituting Socrates' thought.
Adapting Buber's metaphor, I intend not to diminish the role of the
"I" in invention, but to give a needed accent to the inevitable inter-
relationship of I with Thou. The thinking and inventing of any man
or woman happens in large part because of the ways each has interacted with others and with society and culture. The I, as Buber
says, has stood together with others in actuality and, never totally
separate from them even when alone, goes on conversing inwardly,
infinitely.

Our cultural emphasis on individualism in the West which, like so
many things, would be laudable were it not overdone, can be modu-
lated in our teaching about invention if we view it as a social act. No

matter what the academic field or other arena of invention might be, we would be wise to examine not only the fact or result of a discovery, which has typically been credited to one person, but also the evolution of discovery in a social context. We will more fully comprehend the process of creating new ideas when we think of it as an act that is social even as it is individual, with the other always implicated in the inventions of the I.

Notes
Bibliography

Notes

1. Introduction

1. Elbert W. Harrington, *Rhetoric and the Scientific Method of Inquiry: A Study of Invention* (Boulder: Univ. of Colorado Press, 1948), p. 2.
2. Robert Scott et al., "Report of the Committee on the Nature of Rhetorical Invention," in *The Prospect of Rhetoric: Report of the National Development Project*, ed. Lloyd F. Bitzer and Edwin Black (Englewood Cliffs, NJ: Prentice-Hall, 1971), p. 236.
3. Scott et al., p. 229.
4. This rhetorical approach is employed in, for example, S. Michael Halloran's "The Birth of Molecular Biology: An Essay in the Rhetorical Criticism of Scientific Discourse," *Rhetoric Review*, 3 (September 1984), 70–83.
5. Richard E. Young, "Invention: A Topographical Survey," in *Teaching Composition: Ten Bibliographical Essays*, ed. Gary Tate (Fort Worth: Texas Christian Univ. Press, 1979), p. 17.
6. Linda Flower and John R. Hayes, "The Cognition of Discovery: Defining a Rhetorical Problem," *College Composition and Communication*, 31 (February 1980): 21.
7. Ray Bradbury, quoted by Richard Young, Alton Becker, and Kenneth Pike in *Rhetoric: Discovery and Change* (New York: Harcourt Brace Jovanovich, 1970), p. 82.
8. Clarence A. Andrews, *Technical and Business Writing* (Boston: Houghton Mifflin Company, 1975).
9. Herman M. Weisman, *Basic Technical Writing*, 4th ed. (Columbus, OH: Charles E. Merrill Publishing Company, 1980), p. 114.
10. Francis Bacon, *The Works of Francis Bacon*, ed. James Spedding, Robert L. Ellis, and Douglas D. Heath (New York: Hurd and Houghton, 1869, 1963), vol. 6, pp. 268–69. On this point, Elizabeth Eisenstein quotes from E. Harris Harbison's *The Christian Scholar in*

the Age of the Reformation: "Throughout the patristic and medieval periods, the quest for truth is thought of as the recovery of what is embedded in tradition . . . rather than the discovery of what is new," in *The Printing Press as an Agent of Change* vol. 1, (Cambridge and New York: Cambridge Univ. Press, 1979).

11. Peter B. Medawar, *Advice to a Young Scientist* (New York: Harper & Row, 1979), p. 75.

12. Scott et al., pp. 235–36.

13. Douglas Park, "Theories and Expectations: On Conceiving Composition and Rhetoric as a Discipline," *College English*, 41 (September 1979): 52, 54.

2. *A Platonic View of Rhetorical Invention*

1. Martin Buber, *I and Thou*, trans. Walter Kaufman (New York: Charles Scribner's Sons, 1970), p. 115.

2. Lawrence W. Rosenfield, "An Autopsy of the Rhetorical Tradition," in *The Prospect of Rhetoric*, ed. Lloyd Bitzer and Edwin Black (Englewood Cliffs, NJ: Prentice-Hall, 1971), p. 68. Rosenfield cites *The Republic*, pp. 491–96, 532–34; *Theatetus*, pp. 173–74; and the cave allegory as instances in which the aspiring philosopher is said to reject public discourse and proceed on a lonely inner search for a transcendent reality.

3. Plato, *Phaedrus*, trans. W. C. Helmbold and W. G. Rabinowitz (Indianapolis: Bobbs-Merrill, 1977), pp. 30–32.

4. In choosing the term "Platonic invention," I considered and rejected other ways to designate a radically individualistic view of invention. For example, "Neo-Platonic" brings with it unwanted associations with the Renaissance Neo-Platonists and others who fused with Plato certain mystical and religious elements. "Romanticism," another candidate which I rejected, clearly accents the individual as a unique and isolated discoverer of ideas, but its identification with the nineteenth century could imply that the individualistic emphasis dates back only to that point. It seems more appropriate to regard romanticism as a manifestation of an earlier individualistic tradition, one which has continued on to influence twentieth century literary and rhetorical theory.

5. Ralph Waldo Emerson, "The Poet," in *American Literature: Tradition and Innovation*, vol. 1, ed. Harrison Meserole, Walter Sutton, and Brom Weber (Lexington, MA: D. C. Heath and Co., 1969), p. 1010.

6. Ralph Waldo Emerson, "Self Reliance," in Meserole, Sutton, and Weber, pp. 976, 979.

7. Charles Yarnoff, "Contemporary Theories of Invention in the Rhetori-

cal Tradition," *College English*, 41 (January 1980): 553. Subsequent references are cited in the text.

8. Frank J. D'Angelo, *Process and Thought in Composition*, 2nd. ed. (Cambridge, MA: Winthrop, 1980), p. 34. Some of the theorists such as D'Angelo and Elbow, mentioned in this chapter to illustrate Platonic notions, do also attend to certain social aspects of inventing, as is shown in the continuum in chapter 4.

9. Frank J. D'Angelo, *A Conceptual Theory of Rhetoric* (Cambridge, MA: Winthrop, 1975), p. 53.

10. Gordon D. Rohman and Albert O. Wlecke. *Pre-Writing: The Construction and Application of Models for Concept Formation in Writing*, U. S. Office of Education Cooperative Research Project No. 2174, (East Lansing: Michigan State Univ., 1964), ERIC ED001273, p. 56. Subsequent references are cited in the text.

11. D'Angelo, *Conceptual Theory*, p. 52.

12. Gabriele Lusser Rico, *Writing the Natural Way* (Los Angeles: J. P. Tarcher, Inc., 1983), p. 2. Subsequent references are cited in the text.

13. Sidney B. Simon, Robert C. Hawley, and David D. Britton, *Composition for Personal Growth: Values Clarification through Writing* (New York: Hart Publishing Co., 1973), p. 13.

14. Peter Elbow, *Writing with Power* (New York: Oxford Univ. Press, 1981), p. 306.

15. Ken Macrorie, *Telling Writing* (Rochelle Park, NJ: Hayden, 1978), preface.

16. Macrorie, preface.

17. James A. Berlin, "Contemporary Composition: The Major Pedagogical Theories," *College English*, 44 (December 1982): 772. Subsequent references are cited in the text.

18. For an analysis of the dictum to "Be concrete," see Richard Ohmann, "Use Definite, Specific, Concrete Language," *College English*, 41 (December 1979): 390–95. Also, Ohmann's chapter on "Teaching and Studying Literature at the End of Ideology," in his *English in America* (New York: Oxford Univ. Press, 1976), pp. 66–92, discusses the influence of New Critical assumptions on English as a discipline.

19. Alfred Kazin, lecture given on 9 April 1984 at Skidmore College, Saratoga Springs, NY.

20. Terry Eagleton, *Literary Theory: An Introduction* (Oxford: Basil Blackwell, 1983), p. 196.

21. Nicholas Delbanco, *Group Portrait* (New York: William Morrow, 1982); Noel Riley Fitch, *Sylvia Beach and the Lost Generation* (New York: W. W. Norton, 1983).

22. Roland Barthes, *On Racine*, trans. Richard Howard (New York: Hill and Wang, 1964), p. 162.

23. James Kinneavy, "The Relation of the Whole to the Part in Interpretation Theory and in the Composing Process," in *Linguistics, Stylistics, and the Teaching of Composition*, ed. Donald McQuade (Akron, OH: Univ. of Akron, 1979), p. 13.

24. Consider, for example, the following: Christina Baldwin's *One to One: Self-Understanding through Journal Writing* (New York: M. Evans & Co., 1977); Tristine Rainer's *The New Diary: How to Use a Journal for Self-Guidance and Expanded Creativity* (Los Angeles: J. P. Tarcher, Inc., 1978); and Ira Progoff's elaborate Intensive Journal program which is the basis of several books, especially *At a Journal Workshop* (New York: Dialogue House Library, 1975).

25. L. S. Vygotsky, *Thought and Language*, trans. Eugenia Hanfmann and Gertrude Vakar (Cambridge, MA: MIT Press, 1962).

26. A. R. Luria, *Cognitive Development: Its Cultural and Social Foundations*, trans. Martin Lopez-Morrilas and Lynn Solotaroff, ed. Michael Cole (Cambridge, MA: Harvard Univ. Press, 1976). Ironically, Luria's work was suppressed for some time in the Soviet Union, apparently because it was thought that he was criticizing the intelligence of Russian peasants.

27. Elizabeth L. Eisenstein, *The Printing Press as an Agent of Change*, vol. 1 (Cambridge and New York: Cambridge Univ. Press, 1979), pp. 122–25 passim.

28. Daniel J. Boorstin, *The Discoverers* (New York: Random House, 1983), pp. 493, 530.

29. Eisenstein, pp. 120–21.

30. This idea is explored more fully by Ohmann in *English in America*, pp. 316–20.

31. Harold D. Lasswell, "The Social Setting of Creativity," *Creativity and Its Cultivation*, ed. Harold H. Anderson (New York: Harper & Brothers, 1959), p. 205.

32. John W. Gardner, *Self-Renewal: The Individual and the Innovative Society* (New York: Harper & Row, 1971), p. 38.

33. John R. Pierce, "Innovation in Technology," *Scientific American*, 199 (September 1958): 117.

34. Dale Spender, *Women of Ideas (And What Men Have Done to Them)* (London and Boston: Ark Paperbacks, 1983), pp. 44–50.

35. Carol Gilligan, *In a Different Voice* (Cambridge, MA: Harvard Univ. Press, 1982).

36. Patricia Bizzell, "Cognition, Convention, and Certainty: What We Need to Know about Writing," *PRE/TEXT*, 3 (Fall 1982): 215.

37. Bizzell, 239.

38. See, for instance, Lisa Ede and Andrea Lunsford, "Why Write . . . Together?" in *Rhetoric Review*, 1 (January 1983), 150–57. For an update

on research Ede and Lunsford are carrying out on co- and group-authorship, see their "Collaborative Learning: Lessons from the World of Work," *Writing Program Administration,* 9 (Spring 1986): 17–26. Mary Beth Debs' doctoral dissertation (Rensselaer Polytechnic Institute, 1986) is concerned with "Collaboration and Collaborative Writing: A Study of Technical Writing in the Computer Industry." In a different vein, a collection of essays called *Mothering the Mind: Twelve Studies of Writers and Their Silent Partners,* ed. Ruth Perry and Martine Watson Brownley (New York: Holmes & Meier, 1984) studies the relationships of writers with those who nurtured them by acting as critic, mentor, supporter, or muse. Among those discussed are Elizabeth Barrett Browning and Robert Browning, George Eliot and George Henry Lewes, and Gertrude Stein and Alice Toklas.

39. Silvano Arieti, *Creativity: The Magic Synthesis* (New York: Basic Books, Inc., 1976), pp. 307–11.

40. Wayne Booth, *Modern Dogma and the Rhetoric of Assent* (Chicago: Univ. of Chicago Press, 1974), p. 130.

41. Margaret Atwood, *Second Words: Selected Critical Prose* (Toronto: House of Anasi Press Limited, 1982), p. 342.

42. Atwood, pp. 341–2.

43. Alexis de Tocqueville, *Democracy in America,* ed. J. P. Mayer and Max Lerner, trans. George Lawrence (New York: Harper & Row, 1966), p. 478.

44. Philip Slater, *The Pursuit of Loneliness: American Culture at the Breaking Point* (Boston: Beacon Press, 1970), p. 7.

45. Clifford Geertz, *Local Knowledge* (New York: Basic Books, 1983), p. 59.

46. Geertz, pp. 66–67.

47. Georg Simmel, *The Sociology of Georg Simmel,* ed. and trans. Kurt H. Wolff (New York: The Free Press, 1950); George Herbert Mead, *Mind, Self, and Society,* ed. Charles W. Morris (Chicago: Univ. of Chicago Press, 1934); Emile Durkheim, *The Rules of Sociological Method,* trans. Solovay and Mueller (New York: The Free Press, 1966); and Gregory Bateson, *Steps to an Ecology of Mind* (New York: Ballantine, 1972).

48. Booth, *Modern Dogma,* p. 134.

49. S. Michael Halloran, "On Rhetorical Autonomy," paper presented at the Conference on College Composition and Communication, Kansas City, MO, 31 March 1977.

50. Joanna Russ, *How to Suppress Women's Writing* (Austin: Univ. of Texas, 1983), p. 50.

51. Tillie Olsen, *Silences* (New York: Delacorte Press/Seymour Lawrence, 1978), p. 222.

52. John Gardner, interviewed by Pat Ensworth and Joe David Bellamy, in

The New Fiction: Interviews with Innovative American Writers, ed. Joe David Bellamy (Urbana: Univ. of Illinois, 1974), quoted in Olsen, p. 222.

53. John Gardner, quoted in Olsen, p. 222. Questions about contemporary authorship are also raised by ghost-written speeches and so-called autobiographies that are actually written by someone other than the designated author.

54. Thomas S. Kuhn, *The Structure of Scientific Revolutions*, 2nd ed. International Encyclopedia of Unified Science, 2 (Chicago: Univ. of Chicago Press, 1970), p. xi.

3. Invention as a Social Act

1. Max Weber, *The Theory of Social and Economic Organization*, trans. A. M. Henderson and Talcott Parsons (New York: The Free Press, 1947), p. 88.
2. Silvano Arieti, *Creativity: The Magic Synthesis* (New York: Basic Books, Inc., 1976), p. 414. Subsequent references are cited in the text.
3. Lisa S. Ede and Andrea A. Lunsford, "Audience Addressed/Audience Invoked: The Role of Audience in Composition Theory and Pedagogy," *College Composition and Communication*, 35 (May 1984): 158.
4. Ludwik Fleck, *Genesis and Development of a Scientific Fact*, ed. Thaddeus J. Trenn and Robert K. Merton (Basel, Switzerland, 1935; reprint, Chicago: Univ. of Chicago Press, 1979), p. 45.
5. Martin Buber, *I and Thou*, trans. Walter Kaufmann (New York: Charles Scribner's Sons, 1970), p. 115.
6. John Dewey, *The Public and Its Problems* (Denver: Alan Swallow, 1927), p. 24. Subsequent references are cited in the text.
7. I appreciate Richard K. Worthington's assistance in thinking and writing about the relationship of individuals to socioculture.
8. Hannah Arendt, *The Human Condition* (Chicago: Univ. of Chicago Press, 1958), p. 189. Subsequent references are cited in the text.
9. Wayne Booth, *The Rhetoric of Fiction* (Chicago: Univ. of Chicago Press, 1961), p. 90.
10. Janet Wolff, *The Social Production of Art* (New York: St. Martin's, 1981), p. 33.
11. Wolff, p. 33.
12. Margaret Atwood, *Second Words: Selected Critical Prose* (Toronto: House of Anasi Press Limited, 1982), p. 340.
13. Barbara Tuchman, "Biography as a Prism of History," in *Telling Lives: The Biographer's Art*, ed. Marc Pachter (Washington, D.C.: New Republic Books/National Portrait Gallery, 1979), p. 134.

14. See, for example, reports of Donald H. Graves' longitudinal studies of children's writing processes in *A Researcher Learns to Write* (Exeter, NH: Heinemann Educational Books, 1984).

15. Michel Foucault, "The Discourse on Language," in *The Archeology of Knowledge and the Discourse on Language*, trans. A. M. Sheridan Smith (New York: Pantheon, 1982), p. 222. Subsequent references are cited in the text.

16. Fernand Braudel, *On History*, trans. Sarah Matthews (Chicago: Univ. of Chicago Press, 1980), p. 4.

17. Braudel, p. 75.

18. Christopher Gould and Karen Hodges, "The Art of Revision," *Style*, 15 (Spring/Summer 1981): 171.

19. Roger Fisher, "International Mediation," in *To Establish the United States Academy of Peace*, Report of the Commission on Proposals for the National Academy of Peace and Conflict Resolution, #065-000-00116-1 (Washington, D.C.: Government Printing Office, 1982), p. 92.

20. Fisher, pp. 91–94.

21. Richard McKeon, "Love, Self, and Contemporary Culture," in *The Problem of the Self*, ed. P. T. Raju and Alburey Castell (The Hague: Martinus Nijhoff, 1968), p. 16.

22. Aristotle, *Rhetoric*, trans. John Henry Freese, ed. G. P. Goold (Cambridge, MA: Harvard Univ. Press, 1926), 1.3.1358b. Subsequent references are cited in the text.

23. Karlyn Kohrs Campbell, *The Rhetorical Act* (Belmont, CA: Wadsworth, 1982), p. 122.

24. S. Michael Halloran, "Aristotle's Concept of Ethos, or If Not His, Somebody Else's," *Rhetoric Review*, 1 (September 1982): 60.

4. *A Continuum of Social Perspectives on Invention*

1. James Moffett, *Teaching the Universe of Discourse* (Boston: Houghton Mifflin, 1968), p. 33.

2. My thanks to Michael Halloran for this and other insights that helped me in revising an earlier draft of this chapter. T. J. Larkin's comments on various social theorists helped me to develop these theoretical perspectives, and discussions with Lee Odell prompted me to apply the continuum to inventional theories.

3. For a recent (and controversial) discussion, see Jeffrey Masson, *The Assault on Truth: Freud's Suppression of the Seduction Theory* (New York: Farrar, Strauss & Giroux, 1984).

4. Sigmund Freud, *An Outline of Psycho-analysis*, revised ed., trans. James Strachey (New York: W. W. Norton, 1969), pp. 62–63.

5. Albert Rothenberg, *The Emerging Goddess: The Creative Process in Art, Science, and Other Fields* (Chicago: Univ. of Chicago Press, 1979), pp. 139–40. 6. Gerald Holton, "On Trying to Understand Scientific Genius," in Rothenberg, pp. 240–41.

7. Freud, *An Outline of Psycho-analysis*, p. 62.

8. Hannah Arendt, *The Life of the Mind*, 2 vols. (New York: Harcourt Brace Jovanovich, 1978), p. 185.

9. Rudyard Kipling, "Working-Tools," in *The Creative Process: A Symposium*, ed. Brewster Ghiselin (New York: New American Library, 1952), p. 157.

10. Wayne Booth, *Modern Dogma and the Rhetoric of Assent* (Chicago: Univ. of Chicago Press, 1974), p. 126.

11. Charles Horton Cooley, *Human Nature and the Social Order* (New York: Schocken Books, 1964), p. 97.

12. Cooley, p. 119.

13. Harry Stack Sullivan, *The Interpersonal Theory of Psychiatry*, ed. Helen Perry and Mary Garvel (New York: Norton, 1953), p. 239.

14. Sullivan, p. 240.

15. W. H. Auden, *The Dyer's Hand and Other Essays* (New York: Random House, 1968), p. 16.

16. Carl Bereiter and Marlene Scardamalia, "From Conversation to Composition: The Role of Instruction in a Developmental Process," in *Advances in Instructional Psychology*, vol. 2, ed. R. Glaser (Hillsdale, NJ: Lawrence Erlbaum, 1982), 1–64.

17. Lev Semenovich Vygotsky, *Thought and Language*, trans. Eugenia Hanfmann and Gertrude Vakar (Cambridge, MA: M.I.T. Press, 1962). For a discussion of the importance of social speech to thinking and learning (citing Vygotsky, Thomas Kuhn, and Richard Rorty), see Kenneth Bruffee, "Writing and Reading as Collaborative or Social Acts," in *The Writer's Mind: Writing as a Mode of Thinking*, ed. Janice N. Hays, Phyllis A. Roth, Jon R. Ramsey, and Robert D. Foulke (Urbana, IL: NCTE, 1983), pp. 159–70.

18. Linda Flower, "Writer-Based Prose: A Cognitive Basis for Problems in Writing," *College English*, 41 (September 1979): 19–20.

19. Richard E. Young, Alton L. Becker, and Kenneth L. Pike, *Rhetoric: Discovery and Change* (New York: Harcourt Brace Jovanovich, 1970), p. 27.

20. Richard E. Young, "Invention: A Topographical Survey," in *Teaching Composition: Ten Bibliographical Essays*, ed. Gary Tate (Fort Worth: Texas Christian Univ. Press, 1976), p. 23.

21. Charles Yarnoff, "Contemporary Theories of Invention in the Rhetorical Tradition," *College English*, 41 (January 1980): 560. Rogerian argument derives from Carl Roger's client-centered therapy, which has as its

aim the enhancement of the client rather than the solution of mutual problems or the achievement of social change.

22. Described in Richard E. Young, "Theme in Fictional Literature: A Way into Complexity," in *Linguistics, Stylistics, and the Teaching of Composition*, ed. Donald McQuade (Akron, OH: Univ. of Akron, 1979), p. 61.

23. Donald M. Murray, "Writing as Process: How Writing Finds Its Own Meaning," in *Eight Approaches to Teaching Composition*, ed. Timothy R. Donovan and Ben W. McClelland (Urbana, IL: NCTE, 1980), p. 3.

24. Donald Murray, "Writing as Process," p. 12.

25. Donald M. Murray, "Teaching the Other Self: The Writer's First Reader," *College Composition and Communication*, 33 (May 1982): 142.

26. Donald M. Murray, "Teaching the Other Self," 145.

27. Frank J. D'Angelo, "The Dialogue," *Rhetoric Review*, 1 (September 1982): 72.

28. Frank J. D'Angelo, "Paradigms as Structural Counterparts of Topoi," in *Linguistics, Stylistics, and the Teaching of Composition*, ed. Donald McQuade (Akron, OH: Univ. of Akron, 1979), p. 50.

29. Peter Elbow, *Writing with Power* (New York: Oxford Univ. Press, 1981), p. 312. Subsequent references are cited in the text.

30. George Herbert Mead, *Mind, Self and Society*, ed. Charles W. Morris (Chicago: Univ. of Chicago Press, 1934), p. 78.

31. Martin Buber, *I and Thou*, trans. Walter Kaufmann (New York: Charles Scribner's Sons, 1970), p. 80. Subsequent references are cited in the text.

32. Glen Matott, "In Search of a Philosophical Context for Teaching Composition," *College Composition and Communication*, 27 (February 1976): 30.

33. Ludwig Wittgenstein, *Philosophical Investigations*, 3rd ed., trans. G. E. M. Anscombe (New York: Macmillan, 1953), 1:371.

34. Harold D. Lasswell, "The Social Setting of Creativity," *Creativity and Its Cultivation*, ed. Harold H. Anderson (New York: Harper & Brothers, 1959), p. 216. Subsequent references are cited in the text.

35. Silvano Arieti, *Creativity: The Magic Synthesis* (New York: Basic Books, Inc., 1976), p. 293. Subsequent references are cited in the text.

36. Lisa Ede and Andrea Lunsford, "Why Write . . . Together?" *Rhetoric Review*, 1 (January 1983): 155–56.

37. Nicholas Delbanco, *Group Portrait* (New York: William Morrow and Co., 1982), pp. 191–92.

38. Peter Elbow, *Writing without Teachers* (New York: Oxford Univ. Press, 1973).

39. James A. Berlin, "Contemporary Composition: The Major Pedagogical Theories," *College English*, 44 (December 1982): 772.
40. Caroline Gordon to Sally Wood, 21 January 1930 in *The Southern Mandarins: Letters of Caroline Gordon to Sally Wood, 1924–1937*, ed. Sally Wood (Baton Rouge: Louisiana State Univ. Press, 1984), p. 51. The effect of Ford Madox Ford and Allen Tate on Caroline Gordon's process of writing was brought to my attention by Veronica A. Makowsky in a talk on "Caroline Gordon and Allen Tate: What Happens When Your Mentor Is Your Mate," 29 December 1984, Modern Language Association Convention, Washington, D.C.
41. Caroline Gordon to Sally Wood, 30 May 1931, p. 78.
42. Eric Von Hippel, quoted in Thomas J. Peters and Robert H. Waterman, *In Search of Excellence: Lessons from America's Best-Run Companies* (New York: Harper & Row, 1982), p. 194.
43. My source for the summary of synectics in this section was George M. Prince, *The Practice of Creativity* (New York: Macmillan, 1970), p. 34.
44. Henry A. Murray, "Individuality: The Meaning and Content of Individuality in Contemporary America," *Daedalus*, 87 (Spring 1958): 36.
45. The observations about team science in this paragraph come from Alvin M. Weinberg, "Scientific Teams and Scientific Laboratories," *Daedalus*, 99, (Fall 1970): 1069.
46. Kenneth A. Connor, letter to the author, 31 March 1986.
47. Donald Hall, talk given at the University of Vermont, Burlington, VT, 26 October 1978.
48. Ede and Lunsford, "Why Write . . . Together?," pp. 151–53.
49. Philip Spayd, interviewed by author on 14 August 1983 in Ocean City, Maryland.
50. Lewis A. Coser, *Men of Ideas: A Sociologist's View* (New York: The Free Press, 1965), p. 5.
51. Coser, p. 29.
52. Evelyn Fox Keller, *A Feeling for the Organism: The Life and Work of Barbara McClintock* (New York: W. H. Freeman & Co., 1983), p. xv.
53. Keller, pp. 143–51.
54. Delbanco, *Group Portrait*, p. 204.
55. Frances Steloff's memoirs are "In Touch with Genius," *Journal of Modern Literature* (Special Gotham Book Mart Issue), 4 (April 1975).
56. Herbert Marcuse, *One-Dimensional Man* (Boston: Beacon Press, 1964).
57. This explanation of social facts is derived from a discussion in Geoffrey Sampson's *Schools of Linguistics* (Stanford, CA: Stanford Univ. Press, 1980), pp. 44–45. Sampson discusses Durkheim in relation to Saussure, drawing on Durkheim's 1895 *Rules of Sociological Method*, trans.

Solovay and Mueller, New York: The Free Press, 1966. Subsequent references to Sampson are cited in the text.

58. Emile Durkheim, *The Elementary Forms of the Religious Life*, trans. Joseph Ward Swain (Glencoe, IL: The Free Press, 1954), p. 440. Subsequent references are cited in the text.

59. Linda Nochlin, "Why Are There No Great Women Artists?" in *Woman in Sexist Society*, ed. Vivian Gornick and Barbara K. Moran (New York: Basic Books, 1971), p. 488. Subsequent references are cited in the text.

60. My discussion is influenced by Joanna Russ's general arguments on cultural prohibitions in *How to Suppress Women's Writing* (Austin: Univ. of Texas, 1983).

61. Louise Bernikow, ed., *The World Split Open: Four Centuries of Women Poets in England and America, 1552–1950* (New York: Random House, Vintage Books, 1974), p. 16.

62. Bernikow, p. 16.

63. Margaret Rossiter, *Women Scientists in America* (Baltimore, MD: Johns Hopkins Univ. Press, 1982).

64. Benjamin Lee Whorf, *Language, Thought, and Reality*, ed. John B. Carroll (Cambridge, MA: MIT. Press, 1956), p. 247.

65. Adam Schaff, *Language and Cognition*, ed. Robert Cohen (New York: McGraw-Hill, 1973), p. 144.

66. Schaff, p. 144.

67. James L. Adams, *Conceptual Blockbusting: A Guide to Better Ideas* (New York: Norton, 1980), pp. 54–63.

68. Thomas S. Kuhn, *The Structure of Scientific Revolutions*, 2nd ed. International Encyclopedia of Unified Science, 2 (Chicago: Univ. of Chicago Press, 1970), pp. 10, 64.

69. Ludwik Fleck, *Genesis and Development of a Scientific Fact*, ed. Thaddeus J. Trenn and Robert K. Merton (Basel, Switzerland, 1935; reprint Chicago: Univ. of Chicago Press, 1979), p. 39. Subsequent citations are in the text. Carolyn R. Miller's article, "Invention in Technical and Scientific Discourse: A Prospective Survey," in *Research in Technical Communication*, ed. Michael Moran and Debra Journet (Westport, CT: Greenwood Press, 1985), discusses Fleck and Holton and was responsible for leading me to them.

70. Gerald Holton, *The Scientific Imagination* (Cambridge and New York: Cambridge Univ. Press, 1978), p. xi.

71. Paul R. Halmos, "Innovation in Mathematics," *Scientific American*, 199 (September 1958): 71.

72. Virginia Woolf, *A Room of One's Own* (New York: Harcourt, Brace & World, 1929, 1957), pp. 68–69.

73. Woolf, p. 117.

74. T. S. Eliot, "Tradition and the Individual Talent," in *A World of Ideas*, ed. Lee A. Jacobus (New York: St. Martin's, 1983), p. 604.
75. Stephen Jay Gould, "Darwin at Sea—and the Virtues of Port," in *The Flamingo's Smile: Reflections in Natural History* (New York: W. W. Norton, 1985), p. 359.
76. Robert Scott et al., "Report of the Committee on the Nature of Rhetorical Invention," in *The Prospect of Rhetoric: Report of the National Development Project*, ed. Lloyd Bitzer and Edwin Black (Englewood Cliffs, NJ: Prentice-Hall, 1971), p. 230.

5. *The Role of Language: A Foundation for a Social Perspective on Invention*

1. George Steiner, *After Babel* (New York and London: Oxford Univ. Press, 1975), pp. 110, 124. Subsequent references are cited in the text.
2. William Gass, *On Being Blue* (Boston: D. R. Godine, 1976), p. 90.
3. Ernst Cassirer, *The Philosophy of Symbolic Forms*, vol. 1, *Language*, trans. Ralph Manheim (New Haven & London: Yale Univ. Press, 1955; reprint, 1980), p. 87. Subsequent references are cited in the text, abbreviated as *Philosophy* (1). For many discussions that helped me explore the works of Ernst Cassirer in particular and philosophy of language in general, I thank T. J. Larkin, David Brenner, and Douglas Washburn.
4. Ernst Cassirer, *An Essay on Man* (New Haven and London: Yale Univ. Press, 1944; reprint, 1962), p. 130. Subsequent references are cited in the text.
5. Steiner, *After Babel*, pp. 199–200. This seventeenth and eighteenth century desire for a "universal character" that would aid discovery as well as expression of knowledge shows an association of invention with language.
6. Francis Bacon, *Novum Organum*, Book 1, in *Great Books of the Western World*, ed. Robert Maynard Hutchins (Chicago: Encyclopaedia Britannica, Inc., 1952), pp. 107–8.
7. John Amos Comenius, *Orbis Pictus*, trans. Charles Hoole (Syracuse, NY: C. W. Bardeen, 1887), author's preface, p. xvii.
8. Thomas Sprat, *History of the Royal Society*, ed. Jackson I. Cope and Harold Whitmore Jones (St. Louis: Washington Univ. Press, 1959), p. 112.
9. John Locke, *An Essay Concerning Human Understanding*, ed. John Yotton (Cambridge and New York: Cambridge Univ. Press, 1961), Book 3, chapter 9, p. 88.

10. George Berkeley, *A Treatise Concerning the Principles of Human Knowledge*, quoted by Cassirer, *Philosophy* (1), p. 137.
11. John Barth, *The End of the Road* (New York, 1967), p. 147.
12. Carolyn R. Miller concludes that the "windowpane" theory of technical writing is a legacy of a positivist view of science, in "A Humanistic Rationale for Technical Writing," *College English*, 40 (February 1979): 611–12.
13. Antoine Lavoisier, preface to *Elements of Chemistry*, in *Great Books of the Western World*, ed. Robert Maynard Hutchins (Chicago: Encyclopaedia Britannica, 1952), 45:1.
14. John Clifford, "Cognitive Psychology and Writing: A Critique," *Freshman English News*, 13 (Spring 1984): 18.
15. D. Gordon Rohman and Albert O. Wlecke, *Pre-Writing: The Construction and Application of Models for Concept Formation in Writing*, U. S. Office of Education Cooperative Research Project No. 2174 (East Lansing, MI: Michigan State Univ., 1964), ERIC ED001273, p. 58.
16. John S. Fielden, "What Do You Mean I Can't Write?" in *Strategies for Business and Technical Writing*, ed. Kevin J. Harty (New York: Harcourt Brace Jovanovich, 1980), p. 25.
17. Judson Monroe, Carole Meredith, and Kathleen Fisher, *The Science of Scientific Writing* (Dubuque, IA: Kendall Hunt Publishing Co., 1977), p. 59.
18. For a further critique of the "language as conduit" view, see Michael J. Reddy, "The Conduit Metaphor—A Case of Frame Conflict in Our Language about Language," in *Metaphor and Thought*, ed. Andrew Ortony (Cambridge and New York: Cambridge Univ. Press, 1979), pp. 284–324.
19. Jean Piaget, *The Language and Thought of the Child*, trans. Marjorie Gabain (New York: New American Library, 1974), p. 63.
20. Piaget's view is summarized by Donald M. Morehead and Ann Morehead in "From Signal to Sign: A Piagetian View of Thought and Language during the First Two Years," in *Language Perspectives: Acquisition, Retardation, and Intervention*, ed. Richard Schiefelbusch and Lyle Lloyd (Baltimore, MD: Univ. Park Press, 1974), pp. 184–85.
21. Hans G. Furth, "The Influence of Language on the Development of Concept Formation in Deaf Children," *Journal of Abnormal and Social Psychology*, 63 (1961): 389.
22. Albert Einstein, quoted by Jacques Hadamard in *The Psychology of Invention in the Mathematical Field* (Princeton: Princeton Univ. Press, 1949), pp. 142–43.
23. Michael Faraday, *Experimental Researches in Electricity*, in *Great Books of the Western World* (Chicago: Encyclopaedia Britannica, 1952), 45:362.

24. A. B. Arons, "Achieving Wider Scientific Literacy," *Daedalus*, 112 (Spring 1983): 92.

25. Abbe de Condillac, quoted by Lavoisier, preface to *Elements of Chemistry*, p. 1.

26. Lavoisier, p. 1.

27. Lavoisier, in M. P. Crosland, *Historical Studies in the Language of Chemistry* (London: Heinemann, 1962; reprint New York: Dover, 1978), p. 129.

28. Crosland, p. 130.

29. Ernst Cassirer, *The Philosophy of Symbolic Forms*, vol. 3, *The Phenomenology of Knowledge*, trans. Ralph Manheim (New Haven and London: Yale Univ. Press, 1957), p. 331. Hereafter cited in the text, abbreviated as *Philosophy* (3).

30. Lev Semenovich Vygotsky, *Thought and Language*, trans. Eugenia Hanfmann and Gertrude Vakar (Cambridge, MA: MIT Press, 1962), p. 43. Subsequent references are cited in the text.

31. Adam Schaff, *Language and Cognition*, ed. Robert Cohen (New York: McGraw-Hill, 1973), p. 107. Subsequent references are cited in the text.

32. In addition to Hans G. Furth's study cited earlier are the following: *Deafness and Learning: A Psychosocial Approach* (Belmont, CA: Wadsworth, 1973); and, with James Youniss, "Thinking in Deaf Adolescents: Language and Formal Operations," *Journal of Communication Disorders*, 2 (1969): 195–202.

33. Edward Sapir, quoted in Geoffrey Sampson, *Schools of Linguistics* (Stanford, CA: Stanford Univ. Press, 1980), p. 83.

34. Chaim Perelman, "Rhetoric and Philosophy," trans. Henry Johnstone, Jr., *Philosophy and Rhetoric*, 1 (January 1968): 17–18.

35. Immanuel Kant, *Prolegomena to Any Future Metaphysics*, trans. Lewis White Beck, revision of Carus (Indianapolis: Bobbs-Merrill, 1950), p. 99. Subsequent references are cited in the text.

36. Immanuel Kant, *Immanuel Kant's Critique of Pure Reason*, trans. Norman Kemp Smith (London: Macmillan & Co., 1964), p. 172.

37. Wallace Stevens, "So-and-So Reclining on Her Couch," in *The Collected Poems of Wallace Stevens* (New York: Alfred A. Knopf, 1954), pp. 295–96.

38. Jacob Bronowski, *The Ascent of Man* (Boston: Little, Brown and Company, 1973), p. 364.

39. Suzanne Langer, "On Cassirer's Theory of Language and Myth," in *The Philosophy of Ernst Cassirer*, ed. Paul Schilpp (New York: Tudor Pub. Co., 1949), p. 391.

40. S. Michael Halloran and Annette Bradford, "Figures of Speech in the Rhetoric of Science and Technology," in *Essays on Classical Rhetoric and Modern Discourse*, ed. Robert J. Connors, Lisa S. Ede, and An-

drea A. Lunsford (Carbondale: Southern Illinois Univ. Press, 1984), p. 187.

41. Michael Polanyi, *Personal Knowledge: Towards a Post-Critical Philosophy* (New York: Harper & Row, 1964), p. 106.
42. George Lakoff and Mark Johnson, *Metaphors We Live By* (Chicago: Univ. of Chicago Press, 1980), pp. 143–44.
43. Jean Piaget, *To Understand Is to Invent* (New York: Penguin, 1976).
44. Thomas S. Kuhn, "Metaphor in Science," in *Metaphor and Thought*, ed. Andrew Ortony (Cambridge and New York: Cambridge Univ. Press, 1979), p. 418.
45. Julius Laffal, *Pathological and Normal Language* (New York: Atherton Press, 1965), p. 112.
46. Jonathan Culler, *Ferdinand de Saussure*, ed. Frank Kermode (New York: Penguin, 1976), pp. 74–76.
47. George Boas, *The Inquiring Mind* (La Salle, IL: Open Court Publishing Co., 1939), p. 47.
48. Clifford Geertz, *The Interpretation of Cultures* (New York: Basic Books, 1973), p. 360.

6. Implications of a Social Perspective on Rhetorical Invention

1. See, for instance, Kenneth A. Bruffee, "Collaborative Learning: Some Practical Models," in *Ideas for English 101*, ed. Richard Ohmann and W. B. Coley (Urbana, IL: NCTE, 1975), pp. 48–57; Kenneth A. Bruffee, *A Short Course in Writing*, 3rd ed. (Boston: Little, Brown and Co., 1985); and Thom Hawkins, *Group Inquiry Techniques for Teaching Writing* (Urbana, IL: NCTE, 1976).
2. I call attention to several examples of studies of interest at this point primarily for their method and scope, although their findings do have implications as well for our understanding of invention. For research in a college classroom setting, see Anne J. Herrington, "Writing in Academic Settings: A Study of the Contexts for Writing in Two College Chemical Engineering Courses," in *Research in the Teaching of English*, 14 (December 1985): 331–61. For research in an organizational setting, see Lee Odell, "Beyond the Text: Relations Between Writing and Social Context," *Writing in Nonacademic Settings*, ed. Lee Odell and Dixie Goswami (New York: Guilford Publications, 1986): 249–80. A sociocultural approach is being taken by Nan Elsasser and Patricia Irvine in a study of writing in the Virgin Islands, reported in "The Ecology of Literacy," a lecture given at the Fourth International Conference on the Teaching of English, Ottawa, Canada, 14 May 1986. Whether or

not one agrees with the researchers' advocacy of college students' use of
Creole in a society in which standard English is the "official" language,
their approach is notable in that it calls attention to a variety of influences and practices: teacher education; availability of newspapers, li-
braries, and supplies; class and racial divisions affecting the interaction
of faculty and students; informal functions of writing in the society; and
the standardized testing of literacy. For a related report on their experimental writing program at the College of the Virgin Islands, see Nan
Elsasser and Patricia Irvine, "English and Creole: The Dialectics of
Choice in a College Writing Program," *Harvard Educational Review*,
55 (November 1985).

3. Gregory Bateson, *Steps to an Ecology of Mind* (New York: Ballantine,
1972), p. 485.

4. Don Spiegel and Patricia Keith-Spiegel, "Assignment of Publication
Credits: Ethics and Practices of Psychologists," *American Psychologist*,
25 (1970): 744.

5. Dale Spender, *Women of Ideas (And What Men Have Done to Them)*
(London and Boston: Ark Paperbacks, 1983), p. 46.

6. One example of a study of acknowledgments from a feminist perspective is Marilyn Hoder-Salmon, "Collecting Scholars' Wives," *Feminist
Studies*, 4 (October 1978): 107–14.

7. Edward Mendelson, "Authorized Biography and Its Discontents," in
Studies in Biography, ed. Daniel Aaron (Cambridge, MA: Harvard
Univ. Press, 1978), p. 24.

8. Thomas S. Kuhn, *The Structure of Scientific Revolutions*, 2nd ed.,
International Encyclopedia of Unified Science, 2 (Chicago: Univ. of
Chicago Press, 1970), pp. 53–56.

9. Harold D. Lasswell, "The Social Setting of Creativity," in *Creativity
and Its Cultivation*, ed. Harold H. Anderson (New York: Harper and
Brothers, 1959), p. 217.

10. Stephen Jay Gould, "Darwin at Sea—and the Virtues of Port," in *The
Flamingo's Smile: Reflections in Natural History* (New York: W. W. Norton, 1985), p. 347. Kenneth A. Connor suggested this example and contributed in general to my understanding of the role of collaborative activities in invention in science and engineering.

11. Gould, p. 359.

12. Mary Catherine Bateson, *With a Daughter's Eye: A Memoir of Margaret Mead and Gregory Bateson* (New York: William Morrow, 1984),
p. 191. Subsequent references are cited in the text.

13. Richard Ohmann, *English in America* (New York: Oxford Univ. Press,
1976), p. 146.

14. James A. Reither, "Writing and Knowing: Toward Redefining the Writ-

ing Process," *College English*, 47 (October 1985): 625. At the primary school level, students' ethnographic research in the language community is comprehensively described by Shirley Brice Heath in *Ways with Words: Language, Life, and Work in Communities and Classrooms* (Cambridge and New York: Cambridge Univ. Press, 1983). At the college level, I have asked students in a rhetoric and writing course at Rensselaer Polytechnic Institute to work as a research group to investigate the teaching of writing across the curriculum. At St. Thomas University, New Brunswick, Canada, James Reither's undergraduate writing class has worked collaboratively to study what happens when teachers try to teach at the university level, and Russell A. Hunt's students in a course on Restoration and eighteenth century literature carry out a "collaborative investigation" with the aim of writing a textbook on the subject. As described in Hunt's syllabus, this course is also "a course in how to learn about scholarly fields" and, "in effect, a course in writing in various forms, for various audiences, and for various purposes."

15. Ohmann, *English in America*, p. 139.
16. Ewa Pytowska, "Individuality and Collectivity: False Antonyms," in *Absunt Studia in Mores: A Festschrift in Honor of Helga Doblin*, ed. Sarah Stueber Bishop (Saratoga Springs, NY: Skidmore College, 1983), p. 16.
17. The schoolboys of Barbiana give this account of their way of handling visitors' responses to their collectively written pieces: "We call in one outsider after another. We prefer that they not have had too much school. We ask them to read aloud. And we watch to see if they have understood what we meant to say. We accept their suggestions if they clarify the text. We reject any suggestions made in the name of caution." From *Letter to a Teacher from the Schoolboys of Barbiana*, trans. Nora Rossi and Tom Cole (New York: Random House, 1970), pp. 120–22.
18. Richard M. Coe, "Writing in Groups," *Working Teacher*, 2 (1979): 30–31.
19. Frank J. D'Angelo,"The Dialogue," *Rhetoric Review*, 1 (September 1982): 72–80.
20. Tagmemic theory in relation to composition is thoroughly explained in Richard E. Young, Alton L. Becker, and Kenneth L. Pike, *Rhetoric: Discovery and Change* (New York: Harcourt Brace Jovanovich, 1970). A less extensive theoretical framework with a heuristic for considering the relationship of individuals to social context appears in Karen Burke LeFevre and T. J. Larkin's "Freud, Weber, Durkheim: A Philosophical Foundation for Writing in the Humanities and Social Sciences," *Journal of Advanced Composition*, 4, forthcoming.

21. Elaine P. Maimon, Gerald L. Belcher, Gail W. Hearn, Barbara F. Nodine, and Finbarr W. O'Connor, *Readings in the Arts and Sciences* (Boston: Little, Brown, 1984), p. 387.
22. Donald Graves, *A Researcher Learns to Write* (Exeter, NH: Heinemann Educational Books, 1984).
23. Kenneth A. Bruffee, "The Structure of Knowledge and the Future of Liberal Education," *Liberal Education* (Fall 1981): 185. I am indebted to Bruffee's discussion, which influenced my thinking about the relationship of conceptions of knowledge to curricular changes.
24. My summary draws from Bruffee's analysis of changes in twentieth century views of knowledge in "The Structure of Knowledge," pp. 181, 184. The central argument of Kuhn related here comes from *The Structure of Scientific Revolutions*, previously cited.
25. John Gage, "On the Difference between Invention and Pre-Writing," *Freshman English News*, 10 (Fall 1981): 4, 13.
26. Wayne Booth, *Modern Dogma and the Rhetoric of Assent* (Chicago: Univ. of Chicago Press, 1974), p. 141.
27. Booth, p. 149.

BIBLIOGRAPHY

Adams, James L. *Conceptual Blockbusting: A Guide to Better Ideas.* New York: Norton, 1980.

Andrews, Clarence A. *Technical and Business Writing.* Boston: Houghton Mifflin Co., 1975.

Arendt, Hannah. *The Human Condition.* Chicago: Univ. of Chicago Press, 1958.

——. *The Life of the Mind.* 2 vols. New York: Harcourt Brace Jovanovich, 1978.

Arieti, Silvano. *Creativity: The Magic Synthesis.* New York: Basic Books, 1976.

Aristotle. *Rhetoric.* Trans. John Henry Freese. Ed. G. P. Goold. Cambridge, MA: Harvard Univ. Press, 1926.

Arons, A. B. "Achieving Wider Scientific Literacy." *Daedalus,* 112 (Spring 1983): 91–122.

Atwood, Margaret. *Second Words: Selected Critical Prose.* Toronto: House of Anasi Press Limited, 1982.

Auden, W. H. *The Dyer's Hand and Other Essays.* New York: Random House, 1968.

Bacon, Francis. *Novum Organum,* Book 1. In *Great Books of the Western World.* Ed. Robert Maynard Hutchins. Chicago: Encyclopedia Britannica, Inc., 1952.

——. *The Works of Francis Bacon.* Ed. James Spedding, Robert L. Ellis, and Douglas D. Heath. Vol. 6. New York: Hurd and Houghton, 1869, 1963.

Baldwin, Christina. *One-to-One: Self-Understanding Through Journal Writing.* New York: M. Evans & Co., 1977.

Barthes, Roland. *On Racine.* Trans. Richard Howard. New York: Hill and Wang, 1964.

Bateson, Gregory. *Steps to an Ecology of Mind.* New York: Ballantine, 1972.

Bateson, Mary Catherine. *With a Daughter's Eye: A Memoir of Margaret Mead and Gregory Bateson.* New York: William Morrow, 1984.

Bellamy, Joe David, ed. *The New Fiction: Interviews with Innovative American Writers.* Urbana: Univ. of Illinois, 1974.

Bereiter, Carl, and Marlene Scardamalia. "From Conversation to Composition: The Role of Instruction in a Developmental Process." In *Advances in Instructional Psychology.* Ed. R. Glaser. Vol. 2: 1–64. Hillsdale, NJ: Lawrence Erlbaum, 1982.

Berke, Jacqueline. *Twenty Questions for the Writer.* 3rd ed. New York: Harcourt Brace Jovanovich, 1981.

Berlin, James A. "Contemporary Composition: The Major Pedagogical Theories." *College English,* 44 (December 1982): 765–77.

Bernikow, Louise, ed. *The World Split Open: Four Centuries of Women Poets in England and America, 1552–1950.* New York: Random House, Vintage Books, 1974.

Bizzell, Patricia. "Cognition, Convention, and Certainty: What We Need to Know about Writing." *PRE/TEXT,* 3 (Fall 1982): 213–44.

Boas, George. *The Inquiring Mind.* La Salle, IL: Open Court Publishing Co., 1939.

Boorstin, Daniel J. *The Discoverers.* New York: Random House, 1983.

Booth, Wayne C. *Modern Dogma and the Rhetoric of Assent.* Chicago: Univ. of Chicago Press, 1974.

———. *The Rhetoric of Fiction.* Chicago: Univ. of Chicago Press, 1961.

Braudel, Fernand. *On History.* Trans. Sarah Matthews. Chicago: Univ. of Chicago Press, 1980.

Bronowski, Jacob. *The Ascent of Man.* Boston: Little, Brown and Co., 1973.

———. *A Short Course in Writing.* 3rd ed. Boston: Little, Brown and Co., 1985.

Bruffee, Kenneth A. "Collaborative Learning: Some Practical Models." In *Ideas for English 101.* Ed. Richard Ohmann and W. B. Coley, 48–57. Urbana, IL: NCTE, 1975.

———. "Peer Tutoring and the 'Conversation of Mankind.'" In *Writing Centers: Theory and Administration.* Ed. Gary A. Olson, 3–15. Urbana, IL: NCTE, 1984.

———. "The Structure of Knowledge and the Future of Liberal Education." *Liberal Education* (Fall 1981): 177–86.

———. "Writing and Reading as Collaborative or Social Acts." In *The Writer's Mind: Writing as a Mode of Thinking.* Ed. Janice N. Hays, Phyllis A. Roth, Jon R. Ramsey, and Robert D. Foulke, 159–70. Urbana, IL: NCTE, 1983.

Buber, Martin. *I and Thou.* Trans. Walter Kaufmann. New York: Charles Scribner's Sons, 1970.

Burke, Kenneth. *The Philosophy of Literary Form.* Rev. ed. New York: Vintage Books, 1957.

Campbell, Karlyn Kohrs. *The Rhetorical Act.* Belmont, CA: Wadsworth, 1982.

Cassirer, Ernst. *An Essay on Man.* 1944. Reprint. New Haven and London: Yale Univ. Press, 1962.

———. *The Philosophy of Symbolic Forms, Volume 1: Language.* Trans. Ralph Manheim. 1955. Reprint. New Haven and London: Yale Univ. Press, 1980.

———. *The Philosophy of Symbolic Forms, Volume 3. The Phenomenology of Knowledge.* Trans. Ralph Manheim. New Haven and London: Yale Univ. Press, 1957.

Clifford, John. "Cognitive Psychology and Writing: A Critique." *Freshman English News,* 13 (Spring 1984): 16–18.

Coe, Richard M. "Writing in Groups." *Working Teacher,* 2 (1979): 29–31.

Comenius, John Amos. *Orbis Pictus.* Trans. Charles Hoole. Syracuse, NY: C. W. Bardeen, 1887.

Connor, Kenneth A. Letter to the author, 31 March 1986.

Cooley, Charles Horton. *Human Nature and the Social Order.* New York: Schocken Books, 1964.

Coser, Lewis A. *Men of Ideas: A Sociologist's View.* New York: The Free Press, 1965.

Crosland, M. P. *Historical Studies in the Language of Chemistry.* London: Heinemann, 1962. Reprint. New York: Dover, 1978.

Culler, Jonathan. *Ferdinand de Saussure.* Ed. Frank Kermode. New York: Penguin, 1976.

D'Angelo, Frank J. *A Conceptual Theory of Rhetoric.* Cambridge, MA: Winthrop, 1975.

———. "The Dialogue." *Rhetoric Review,* 1 (September 1982): 72–80.

———. "Paradigms as Structural Counterparts of Topoi." In *Linguistics, Stylistics, and the Teaching of Composition.* Ed. Donald McQuade, 41–51. Akron, OH: Univ. of Akron, 1979.

————. *Process and Thought in Composition*. 2nd ed. Cambridge, MA: Winthrop, 1980.

Debs, Mary Beth. "Collaboration and Collaborative Writing: A Study of Technical Writing in the Computer Industry." Unpublished Ph.D. dissertation, Rensselaer Polytechnic Institute, 1986.

Delbanco, Nicholas. *Group Portrait*. New York: William Morrow, 1982.

Dewey, John. *The Public and Its Problems*. Denver: Alan Swallow, 1927.

Durkheim, Emile. *The Elementary Forms of Religious Life*. Trans. Joseph Ward Swain. Glencoe, IL: The Free Press, 1954.

————. *The Rules of Sociological Method*. Trans. Solovay and Mueller. New York: The Free Press, 1966.

Eagleton, Terry. *Literary Theory: An Introduction*. Oxford: Basil Blackwell, 1983.

Ede, Lisa S., and Andrea A. Lunsford. "Audience Addressed/Audience Invoked: The Role of Audience in Composition Theory and Pedagogy." *College Composition and Communication*, 35 (May 1984): 155–71.

————. "Collaborative Learning: Lessons from the World of Work." *Writing Program Administration*, 9 (Spring 1986): 17–26.

————. "Why Write . . . Together?" *Rhetoric Review*, 1 (January 1983): 150–57.

Eisenstein, Elizabeth L. *The Printing Press as an Agent of Change*. Vol. 1. Cambridge and New York: Cambridge Univ. Press, 1979.

Elbow, Peter. *Writing without Teachers*. New York: Oxford Univ. Press, 1973.

————. *Writing with Power*. New York: Oxford Univ. Press, 1981.

Eliot, T. S. "Tradition and the Individual Talent." In *A World of Ideas*. Ed. Lee A. Jacobus, 599–614. New York: St. Martin's, 1983.

Elsasser, Nan, and Patricia Irvine. "The Ecology of Literacy." Lecture given at the Fourth International Conference on the Teaching of English, Ottawa, Canada, 14 May 1986.

————. "English and Creole: The Dialectics of Choice in a College Writing Program." *Harvard Educational Review*, 55 (November 1985).

Emerson, Ralph Waldo. "The Poet." In *American Literature: Tradition and Innovation*. Vol. 1. Ed. Harrison Meserole, Walter Sutton, and Brom Weber. 994–1011. Lexington, MA: D. C. Heath and Co., 1969.

————. "Self Reliance." In *American Literature: Tradition and Innovation*. Vol. 1. Ed. Harrison Meserole, Walter Sutton, and Brom Weber, 976–94. Lexington, MA: D. C. Heath and Co., 1969.

Faraday, Michael. *Experimental Researches in Electricity.* Vol. 45. In *Great Books of the Western World.* Chicago: Encyclopaedia Britannica, 1952.

Fielden, John S. "What Do You Mean I Can't Write?" In *Strategies for Business and Technical Writing.* Ed. Kevin J. Harty, 14–28. New York: Harcourt Brace Jovanovich, 1980.

Fish, Stanley. *Is There a Text in This Class?* Cambridge, MA: Harvard Univ. Press, 1980.

Fisher, Roger. "International Mediation." In *To Establish the United States Academy of Peace,* 90–96. Report of the Commission on Proposals for the National Academy of Peace and Conflict Resolution, (#065-000-00116-1). Washington, D.C.: Government Printing Office, 1982.

Fisher, Roger, and William Ury. *Getting to Yes: Negotiating Agreement without Giving In.* New York: Penguin Books, 1983.

Fitch, Noel Riley. *Sylvia Beach and the Lost Generation.* New York: W. W. Norton, 1983.

Fleck, Ludwik. *Genesis and Development of a Scientific Fact.* Basel, Switzerland, 1935. Reprint. Ed. Thaddeus J. Trenn and Robert K. Merton. Chicago: Univ. of Chicago Press, 1979.

Flower, Linda. "Writer-Based Prose: A Cognitive Basis for Problems in Writing." *College English,* 41 (September 1979): 19–37.

Flower, Linda, and John R. Hayes. "The Cognition of Discovery: Defining a Rhetorical Problem." *College Composition and Communication,* 31 (February 1980): 21–32.

Foucault, Michel. "The Discourse on Language." In *The Archeology of Knowledge and the Discourse on Language.* Trans. A. M. Sheridan Smith. New York: Pantheon, 1982. 215–38.

Freud, Sigmund. *An Outline of Psycho-analysis.* Rev. ed. Trans. James Strachey. New York: W. W. Norton, 1969.

Furth, Hans G. *Deafness and Learning: A Psychosocial Approach.* Belmont, CA: Wadsworth, 1973.

———. "The Influence of Language on the Development of Concept Formation in Deaf Children." *Journal of Abnormal and Social Psychology,* 63 (1961): 386–89.

Furth, Hans G., and James Youniss. "Thinking in Deaf Adolescents: Language and Formal Operations." *Journal of Communication Disorders,* 2 (1969): 195–202.

Gage, John. "On the Difference between Invention and Pre-Writing." *Freshman English News,* 10 (Fall 1981): 4–14.

Gardner, John. *On Becoming a Novelist*. New York: Harper & Row, 1983.

Gardner, John W. *Self-Renewal: The Individual and the Innovative Society*. New York: Harper & Row, 1971.

Gass, William. *On Being Blue*. Boston: D. R. Godine, 1976.

Geertz, Clifford. *The Interpretation of Cultures*. New York: Basic Books, 1973.

———. *Local Knowledge*. New York: Basic Books, 1983.

Gilligan, Carol. *In a Different Voice*. Cambridge, MA: Harvard Univ. Press, 1982.

Gordon, Caroline. *The Southern Mandarin: Letters of Caroline Gordon to Sally Wood, 1924–1937*. Ed. Sally Wood. Baton Rouge: Louisiana State Univ. Press, 1984.

Gould, Christopher and Karen Hodges, "The Art of Revision." *Style*, 15 (Spring/Summer 1981): 171–221.

Gould, Stephen Jay. "Darwin at Sea—and the Virtues of Port." In *The Flamingo's Smile: Reflections in Natural History*, 347–59. New York: W. W. Norton, 1985.

Graves, Donald H. *A Researcher Learns to Write*. Exeter, NH: Heinemann Educational Books, 1984.

Hadamard, Jacques. *The Psychology of Invention in the Mathematical Field*. Princeton: Princeton Univ. Press, 1949.

Hall, Donald. Lecture at the Univ. of Vermont, Burlington, Vermont, 26 October 1978.

Halloran, S. Michael. "Aristotle's Concept of Ethos, or If Not His, Somebody Else's." *Rhetoric Review*, 1 (September 1982): 58–63.

———. "The Birth of Molecular Biology: An Essay in the Rhetorical Criticism of Scientific Discourse." *Rhetoric Review*, 3 (September 1984): 70–83.

———. "On Rhetorical Autonomy." Paper presented at the Conference on College Composition and Communication. Kansas City, MO, 31 March 1977.

———. "Technical Writing and the Rhetoric of Science." *Journal of Technical Writing and Communication*, 8 (1978): 77–88.

Halloran, S. Michael, and Annette Bradford. "Figures of Speech in the Rhetoric of Science and Technology." In *Essays on Classical Rhetoric and Modern Discourse*. Ed. Robert J. Connors, Lisa S. Ede, and Andrea A. Lunsford, 179–92. Carbondale: Southern Illinois Univ. Press, 1984.

Halmos, Paul R. "Innovation in Mathematics." *Scientific American*, 199 (September 1958): 66–73.

Harrington, Elbert W. *Rhetoric and the Scientific Method of Inquiry: A Study of Invention.* Univ. of Colorado Studies, Series in Language and Literature. Boulder: Univ. of Colorado Press, 1948.

Hawkins, Thom. *Group Inquiry Techniques for Teaching Writing.* Urbana, IL: NCTE, 1976.

Heath, Shirley Brice. *Ways with Words: Language, Life, and Work in Communities and Classrooms.* Cambridge and New York: Cambridge Univ. Press, 1983.

Herrington, Anne J. "Writing in Academic Settings: A Study of the Contexts for Writing in Two College Chemical Engineering Courses." *Research in the Teaching of English,* 14 (December 1985): 331–61.

Hoder-Salmon, Marilyn. "Collecting Scholars' Wives." *Feminist Studies,* 4 (October 1978): 107–14.

Holton, Gerald. *The Scientific Imagination.* Cambridge and New York: Cambridge Univ. Press, 1978.

Kant, Immanuel. *Immanuel Kant's Critique of Pure Reason.* Trans. Norman Kemp Smith. London: Macmillan & Co., 1964.

———. *Prolegomena to Any Future Metaphysics.* Trans. Lewis White Beck, revision of Carus. Indianapolis: Bobbs-Merrill, 1950.

Kazin, Alfred. Lecture at Skidmore College, Saratoga Springs, NY, 9 April 1984.

Keller, Evelyn Fox. *A Feeling for the Organism: The Life and Work of Barbara McClintock.* New York: W. H. Freeman & Co., 1983.

Kinneavy, James. "The Relation of the Whole to the Part in Interpretation Theory and in the Composing Process." In *Linguistics, Stylistics, and the Teaching of Composition.* Ed. Donald McQuade, 1–23. Akron, OH: Univ. of Akron, 1979.

Kipling, Rudyard. "Working-Tools." In *The Creative Process: A Symposium.* Ed. Brewster Ghiselin, 157–58. New York: New American Library, 1952.

Kuhn, Thomas S. "Metaphor in Science." In *Metaphor and Thought.* Ed. Andrew Ortony, 409–19. Cambridge and New York: Cambridge Univ. Press, 1979.

———. *The Structure of Scientific Revolutions.* 2nd ed. International Encyclopedia of Unified Science, 2. Chicago: Univ. of Chicago Press, 1970.

Laffal, Julius. *Pathological and Normal Language.* New York: Atherton Press, 1965.

Lakoff, George, and Mark Johnson. *Metaphors We Live By.* Chicago: Univ. of Chicago Press, 1980.

Langer, Suzanne. "On Cassirer's Theory of Language and Myth." In *The*

Philosophy of Ernst Cassirer. Ed. Paul Schilpp, 381–400. New York: Tudor Publishing Co., 1949.

Larson, Richard L. "A Plan for Teaching Rhetorical Invention." *College English*, 30 (November 1968): 126–34. Reprinted in Edward P. J. Corbett, *Classical Rhetoric for the Modern Student*, 163–67. 2nd ed. New York: Oxford Univ. Press, 1971.

Lasswell, Harold D. "The Social Setting of Creativity." In *Creativity and Its Cultivation.* Ed. Harold H. Anderson, 203–21. New York: Harper & Brothers, 1959.

Lavoisier, Antoine. *Elements of Chemistry.* In *Great Books of the Western World.* Ed. Robert Maynard Hutchins. Chicago: Encyclopaedia Britannica, 1952.

LeFevre, Karen Burke, and T. J. Larkin. "Freud, Weber, and Durkheim: A Philosophical Foundation for Writing in the Humanities and Social Sciences." *Journal of Advanced Composition*, 4, forthcoming.

Lenneberg, Eric H. *Biological Foundations of Language.* New York: Wiley, 1967.

Locke, John. *An Essay Concerning Human Understanding.* Ed. John Yotton. Cambridge and New York: Cambridge Univ. Press, 1961.

Luria, A. R. *Cognitive Development: Its Cultural and Social Foundations.* Trans. Martin Lopez-Morrilas and Lynn Solotaroff. Ed. Michael Cole. Cambridge, MA: Harvard Univ. Press, 1976.

McKeon, Richard. "Love, Self, and Contemporary Culture." In *The Problem of the Self.* Ed. P. T. Raju and Alburey Castell, 13–33. The Hague: Martinus Nijhoff, 1968.

Macrorie, Ken. *Telling Writing.* Rochelle Park, NJ: Hayden, 1978.

Maimon, Elaine, Gerald L. Belcher, Gail W. Hearn, Barbara F. Nodine, and Finbarr W. O'Connor. *Readings in the Arts and Sciences.* Boston: Little, Brown and Co., 1984.

Makowsky, Veronica. "Caroline Gordon and Allen Tate: What Happens When Your Mentor Is Your Mate," Lecture at the Modern Language Association Convention, Washington, D.C., 29 December 1984.

Marcuse, Herbert. *One-Dimensional Man.* Boston: Beacon Press, 1964.

Masson, Jeffrey. *The Assault on Truth: Freud's Suppression of the Seduction Theory.* New York: Farrar, Strauss & Giroux, 1984.

Matott, Glenn. "In Search of a Philosophical Context for Teaching Composition." *College Composition and Communication*, 27 (February 1976): 25–31.

Mead, George Herbert. *Mind, Self, and Society*. Ed. Charles W. Morris. Chicago: Univ. of Chicago Press, 1934.

Medawar, Peter B. *Advice to a Young Scientist*. New York: Harper & Row, 1979.

Mendelson, Edward. "Authorized Biography and Its Discontents." In *Studies in Biography*. Ed. Daniel Aaron, 9–26. Cambridge, MA: Harvard Univ. Press, 1978.

Miller, Carolyn R. "A Humanistic Rationale for Technical Writing." *College English*, 40 (February 1979): 610–17.

――――. "Invention in Technical and Scientific Discourse: A Prospective Survey." In *Research in Technical Communication*. Ed. Michael G. Moran and Debra Journet, 117–161. Westport, CT: Greenwood Press, 1985.

Moffett, James. *Teaching the Universe of Discourse*. Boston: Houghton Mifflin, 1968.

Monroe, Judson, Carole Meredith, and Kathleen Fisher. *The Science of Scientific Writing*. Dubuque, IA: Kendall Hunt Publishing Co., 1977.

Morehead, Donald M., and Ann Morehead. "From Signal to Sign: A Piagetian View of Thought and Language during the First Two Years." In *Language Perspectives: Acquisition, Retardation, and Intervention*. Ed. Richard Schiefelbusch and Lyle Lloyd. Baltimore, MD: Univ. Park Press, 1974.

Murray, Donald M. "The Feel of Writing―and Teaching Writing." In *Reinventing the Rhetorical Tradition*. Ed. Aviva Freedman and Ian Pringle, 67–74. Conway, AR: L & S Books, 1980.

――――. "Internal Revision: A Process of Discovery." In *Research on Composing*. Ed. Charles R. Cooper and Lee Odell, 85–104. Urbana, IL: NCTE, 1978.

――――. "Teaching the Other Self: The Writer's First Reader." *College Composition and Communication*, 33 (May 1982): 140–47.

――――. "Writing as Process: How Writing Finds Its Own Meaning." In *Eight Approaches to Teaching Composition*. Ed. Timothy R. Donovan and Ben W. McClelland, 3–20. Urbana, IL: NCTE, 1980.

Murray, Henry A. "Individuality: The Meaning and Content of Individuality in Contemporary America." *Daedalus*, 87 (Spring 1958): 25–47.

Nochlin, Linda. "Why Are There No Great Women Artists?" *Woman in Sexist Society*. Ed. Vivian Gornick and Barbara K. Moran, 480–510. New York: Basic Books, 1971.

Odell, Lee. "Beyond the Text: Relations between Writing and Social Context." In *Writing in Nonacademic Settings.* Ed. Lee Odell and Dixie Goswami, 249–80. New York: Guilford Publications, 1986.

Odell, Lee, and Dixie Goswami. "Writing in a Nonacademic Setting." *Research in the Teaching of English,* 16 (October 1982): 201–24.

Ohmann, Richard. *English in America.* New York: Oxford Univ. Press, 1976.

———. "Use Definite, Specific, Concrete Language." *College English,* 41 (December 1979): 390–95.

Olsen, Tillie. *Silences.* New York: Delacorte Press/Seymour Lawrence, 1978.

Park, Douglas. "Theories and Expectations: On Conceiving Composition and Rhetoric as a Discipline." *College English,* 41 (September 1979): 46–56.

Perelman, Chaim. "Rhetoric and Philosophy." Trans. Henry W. Johnstone, Jr., *Philosophy and Rhetoric,* 1 (January 1968): 15–23.

Perry, Ruth, and Martine Watson Brownley, eds. *Mothering the Mind: Twelve Studies of Writers and Their Silent Partners.* New York: Holmes & Meier, 1984.

Peters, Thomas J., and Robert H. Waterman. *In Search of Excellence: Lessons From America's Best-Run Companies.* New York: Harper & Row, 1982.

Piaget, Jean. *The Language and Thought of the Child.* Trans. Marjorie Gabain. New York: New American Library, 1974.

———. *To Understand Is to Invent.* New York: Penguin, 1976.

Pierce, John R. "Innovation in Technology." *Scientific American,* 199 (September 1958): 117–30.

Plato. *Phaedrus.* Trans. W. C. Helmbold and W. G. Rabinowitz. Indianapolis: Bobbs-Merrill, 1977.

Polanyi, Michael. *Personal Knowledge: Towards a Post-Critical Philosophy.* New York: Harper & Row, 1964.

Prince, George M. *The Practice of Creativity.* New York: Macmillan, 1970.

Progoff, Ira. *At a Journal Workshop.* New York: Dialogue House Library, 1975.

Pytowska, Ewa. "Individuality and Collectivity: False Antonyms." In *Abeunt Studia in Mores: A Festschrift in Honor of Helga Doblin.* Ed. Sarah Stueber Bishop. Saratoga Springs, NY: Skidmore College, 1983.

Rainer, Tristine. *The New Diary: How to Use a Journal for Self-Guidance and Expanded Creativity.* Los Angeles: J. P. Tarcher, Inc., 1978.

Reddy, Michael J. "The Conduit Metaphor—A Case of Frame Conflict in Our Language about Language." In *Metaphor and Thought*, ed. Andrew Ortony. Cambridge and New York: Cambridge Univ. Press, 1971.

Reither, James A. "Writing and Knowing: Toward Redefining the Writing Process." *College English*, 47 (October 1985): 620–28.

Rico, Gabriele Lusser. *Writing the Natural Way.* Los Angeles: J. P. Tarcher, Inc., 1983.

Riegel, Klaus. *Foundations of Dialectical Psychology.* New York: Academic Press, 1979.

———. "The Influence of Economic and Political Ideologies on the Development of Developmental Psychology." *Psychological Bulletin*, 78 (1972): 129–41.

Rohman, D. Gordon, and Albert O. Wlecke. *Pre-Writing: The Construction and Application of Models for Concept Formation in Writing.* U.S. Office of Education Cooperative Research Project No. 2174. East Lansing: Michigan State Univ., 1964. ERIC ED001273.

Rosenblatt, Louise M. *The Reader, the Text, the Poem.* Carbondale: Southern Illinois Univ. Press, 1978.

Rosenfield, Lawrence W. "An Autopsy of the Rhetorical Tradition." In *The Prospect of Rhetoric.* Ed. Lloyd Bitzer and Edwin Black, 64–77. Englewood Cliffs, NJ: Prentice-Hall, 1971.

Rossi, Nora, and Tom Cole, trans. *Letter to a Teacher from the Schoolboys of Barbiana.* New York: Random House, 1970.

Rossiter, Margaret. *Women Scientists in America.* Baltimore, MD: Johns Hopkins Univ. Press, 1982.

Rothenberg, Albert. *The Emerging Goddess: The Creative Process in Art, Science, and Other Fields.* Chicago: Univ. of Chicago Press, 1979.

Russ, Joanna. *How to Suppress Women's Writing.* Austin: Univ. of Texas Press, 1983.

Sampson, Geoffrey. *Schools of Linguistics.* Stanford, CA: Stanford Univ. Press, 1980.

Schaff, Adam. *Language and Cognition.* Ed. Robert Cohen. New York: McGraw-Hill, 1973.

Scott, Robert, James R. Andrews, Howard H. Martin, J. Richard McNally, William F. Nelson, Michael M. Osborn, Arthur L. Smith, and Harold

Zyskind. "Report of the Committee on the Nature of Rhetorical Invention." In *The Prospect of Rhetoric: Report of the National Development Project*. Ed. Lloyd F. Bitzer and Edwin Black, 228–236. Englewood Cliffs, NJ: Prentice-Hall, 1971.

Simmel, Georg. *The Sociology of Georg Simmel*. Ed. and trans. Kurt H. Wolff. New York: The Free Press, 1950.

Simon, Sidney B., Robert C. Hawley, and David D. Britton. *Composition for Personal Growth: Values Clarification through Writing*. New York: Hart Publishing Co., 1973.

Slater, Philip. *The Pursuit of Loneliness: American Culture at the Breaking Point*. Boston: Beacon Press, 1970.

Spayd, Philip. Interview with the author. Ocean City, Maryland, 14 August 1983.

Spender, Dale. *Women of Ideas (And What Men Have Done to Them)*. London and Boston: Ark Paperbacks, 1983.

Spiegel, Don, and Patricia Keith-Spiegel. "Assignment of Publication Credits: Ethics and Practices of Psychologists." *American Psychologist*, 25 (1970): 738–47.

Sprat, Thomas. *History of the Royal Society*. Ed. Jackson I. Cope and Harold Whitmore Jones. St. Louis: Washington Univ. Press, 1959.

Steiner, George. *After Babel*. New York and London: Oxford Univ. Press, 1975.

Stevens, Wallace. *The Collected Poems of Wallace Stevens*. New York: Alfred A. Knopf, 1954.

Sullivan, Harry Stack. *The Interpersonal Theory of Psychiatry*. Ed. Helen Perry and Mary Garvel. New York: Norton, 1953.

Tocqueville, Alexis de. *Democracy in America*. Ed. J. P. Mayer and Max Lerner. Trans. George Lawrence. New York: Harper & Row, 1966.

Tuchman, Barbara. "Biography as a Prism of History." In *Telling Lives: The Biographer's Art*. Ed. Marc Pachter, 132–147. Washington, D.C.: New Republic Books/National Portrait Gallery, 1979.

Vygotsky, Lev Semenovich. *Thought and Language*. Trans. Eugenia Hanfmann and Gertrude Vakar. Cambridge, MA: MIT Press, 1962.

Weber, Max. *The Methodology of the Social Sciences*. Trans. and ed. Edward A. Shils and Henry A. Finch. New York: The Free Press, 1949.

———. *The Theory of Social and Economic Organization*. Trans. A. M. Henderson and Talcott Parsons. New York: The Free Press, 1947.

Weinberg, Alvin M. "Scientific Teams and Scientific Laboratories." *Daedalus*, 99 (Fall 1970): 1056–75.

Weisman, Herman M. *Basic Technical Writing*. 4th ed. Columbus, OH: Charles E. Merrill Publishing Company, 1980.

Whorf, Benjamin Lee. *Language, Thought, and Reality*. Ed. John B. Carroll. Cambridge, MA: MIT Press, 1956.

Wilson, R. R. "My Fight against Team Research." *Daedalus*, 99 (Fall 1970): 1076–87.

Wittgenstein, Ludwig. *Philosophical Investigations*. 3rd ed. Trans. G. E. M. Anscombe. New York: Macmillan, 1953.

Wolff, Janet. *The Social Production of Art*. New York: St. Martin's, 1981.

Woolf, Virginia. *A Room of One's Own*. New York: Harcourt, Brace & World, 1929, 1957.

Yarnoff, Charles. "Contemporary Theories of Invention in the Rhetorical Tradition." *College English*, 41 (January 1980): 552–60.

Young, Richard E. "Invention: A Topographical Survey." In *Teaching Composition: Ten Bibliographical Essays*. Ed. Gary Tate, 1–43. Fort Worth: Texas Christian Univ. Press, 1976.

———. "Paradigms and Problems: Needed Research in Rhetorical Invention." In *Research on Composing*. Ed. Charles R. Cooper and Lee Odell, 29–48. Urbana, IL: NCTE, 1978.

———. "Theme in Fictional Literature: A Way into Complexity." *Linguistics, Stylistics, and the Teaching of Composition*. Ed. Donald McQuade, 61–71. Akron, OH: Univ. of Akron, 1979.

Young, Richard E., Alton L. Becker, and Kenneth L. Pike. *Rhetoric: Discovery and Change*. New York: Harcourt Brace Jovanovich, 1970.

KAREN BURKE LEFEVRE is director of the Writing Center and assistant professor of rhetoric and composition at Rensselaer Polytechnic Institute in Troy, New York. She is coauthor with Mary Jane Dickerson of *Until I See What I Say: Teaching Writing in All Disciplines* (University of Vermont, 1981). Her research interests include invention, writing across the curriculum, and the social aspects of rhetoric, composition, and literature. She lives in Burlington, Vermont.